QUIZ WHIZ

HISTORY

2/1

QUIZ WHIZ
HISTORY

KINGFISHER

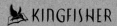
KINGFISHER

First published 2011 by Kingfisher
an imprint of Macmillan Children's Books
a division of Macmillan Publishers Limited
20 New Wharf Road, London N1 9RR
Basingstoke and Oxford
Associated companies throughout the world
www.panmacmillan.com

ISBN 978-0-7534-3221-1

Copyright © Macmillan Children's Books 2011
Produced for Kingfisher by Toucan Books Ltd

9 8 7 6 5 4 3 2 1
1TR/0711/WKT/UNTD/140MA

A CIP catalogue record for this book is available from the British Library.

Printed in China

Author: Dr Jacob Field

Contents

Orville and Wilbur Wright and their 'Flyer'

How to use this book

Read all about it first! Start with the introduction and follow the boxes across the pages from left to right and top to bottom. Look at the pictures, too, because sometimes the answers can be found there. Then it is time to tackle the questions...

1. Eight questions

The questions are on the far left. In addition to general questions, there are true or false options and sometimes you have to unjumble letters to find the answer!

2. Follow the numbers!

All the answers are somewhere on the page. If you do not know the answer straight away, each question has a matching number in a coloured circle to help you find the right place to read.

3. Find the answer

When you have answered all the questions, turn to the back of the book and see if you were right!

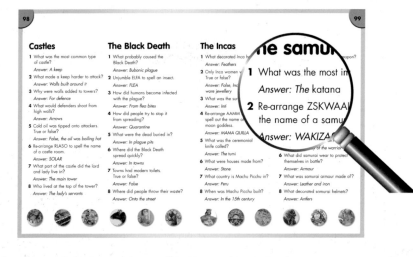

Chapter one
PREHISTORY
4.5 million years ago – 5000BCE

First humans

The first humans appeared more than two million years ago, but they would have looked very different from people today! After thousands of years, they evolved into modern humans like us who are known as *Homo sapiens*.

1 Where did *Homo sapiens* first live?

2 When did *Homo sapiens* first leave Africa?

3 Where did *Homo sapiens* go next?

4 What animal group does EARMPTIS spell?

5 What is *Homo sapiens'* closest living relation?

6 What was the first type of human called?

7 Was fruit eaten by early humans?

8 *Homo habilis* ate meat. True or false?

Homo habilis

Homo sapiens　　1 2 3
Homo sapiens first appeared in the continent of Africa. About 50,000 years ago they began to move across the rest of the world. First they went to Oceania and southeast Asia, and then went on to populate almost every corner of the planet.

1 *Ardipithecus* **2** *Australopithecus* **3** *Homo habilis* **4** *Homo erectus* **5** *Homo sapiens*

Evolution 4 5 6

We evolved from apes and are part of an animal group called 'primates'. This group includes chimpanzees, our closest living relation. The first type of human was called *Homo habilis*.

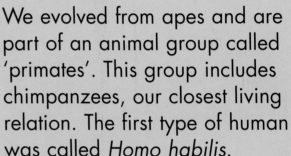

Gathering food 7 8

Australopithecus could walk upright. They mostly ate fruit, berries and roots. Later, *Homo habilis* added meat to their diet. They took this from the bodies of animals killed by predators.

Niandatroles

Early tools

The first humans made simple stone tools. As early humans evolved, species such as *Homo erectus* began to create more complicated tools.

1 When did humans first begin making tools?

2 Who made the first tools?

3 What were the first tools used for?

4 Re-arrange NAHD XEA to spell a hunting tool.

5 What did *Homo erectus* use to shape stone tools?

6 When did the Neanderthals emerge?

7 What was a borer used for?

8 Tools were not used to make fire. True or false?

First tools

1 2 3

The first tools were made more than two million years ago by *Homo habilis*. They made simple tools by hitting stones together to make sharp edges. They used these tools for chopping meat and digging up roots.

simple stone tool

First hunters 4 5

Homo erectus were probably the first humans to hunt. They made a tool called a hand axe to help them. *Homo erectus* used wood or bone to shape stones into much sharper tools.

using a tool to skin an animal

MAKING A HAND AXE

hammerstone

core

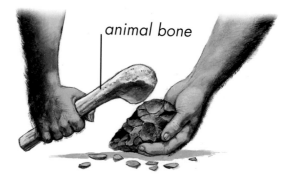

animal bone

1 *A hammerstone was used to break off pieces from the flint (core)*

2 *Smaller pieces were then broken off to create a rough oval shape*

3 *The axe was sharpened by chipping at the stone with a piece of animal bone*

Neanderthals 6 7

The Neanderthals emerged around 100,000 years ago. They used many different types of tool. The Neanderthals made sharp knives out of flint, a hard and flakey stone. They also used a borer to make holes in animal skins.

 flint knife   *borer*

Making a fire 8

Homo erectus were the first to use tools to help create fire. One way this was done was to strike a piece of flint against a stone. This would make sparks.

At home

Over time, humans began to live in larger settlements, rather than in small family groups. A number of families lived together in a settlement and helped each other get food.

1 What shape were shelters?

2 What animal's bones held up the shelters?

3 What material covered the shelters?

4 Where was meat cooked?

5 How did people grind seeds?

6 Where was the first baking done?

7 Humans painted wild animals on cave walls. True or false?

8 Re-arrange RCHOE to spell a coloured clay.

Village life in Siberia   1 2 3 4
A People lived in circular shelters.
B The bones of large animals, such as the woolly mammoth, held up the shelters.
C The bones were covered with animal skins to keep out the wind, rain and cold.
D Hunters cooked meat on a spit.
E People gathered wood to feed the fire.
F Mammoth bones are large and heavy.

Making bread (5)(6)

Bread took a long time to make. People gathered grass and separated out the seeds. Then they used a heavy stone to grind the seeds to make flour. They mixed the flour with water and baked it to make bread dough. The first baking was done on hot stones or in the ashes of a fire.

C

F

Cave painting (7)(8)

People began painting on cave walls more than 30,000 years ago. Wild animals such as horses and bison were the most common subject. They used natural materials such as charcoal and clay as paint. Charcoal made black or grey marks. Ochre is a kind of coloured clay. It can be red or yellow.

Hunting

For many thousands of years, people have hunted animals for food. As better weapons were created, early humans hunted larger animals, such as the mighty woolly mammoth.

1 A spear is sharp. True or false?

2 Did people hunt large animals alone?

3 The mammoth is the size of what modern animal?

4 What parts of the woolly mammoth did people use?

5 Fish hooks were made of what?

6 Unjumble RHOAPNO to spell a tool.

7 When was the bow and arrow first used?

8 What did it allow people to do?

hunting axe

1 spear

Big game ② ③ ④
To hunt large animals, people had to work together. The woolly mammoth was the size of an elephant. Mammoths provided meat. People also used the skins and tusks. They made clothes and shelters from them.

Fishing 5

Fish were caught by spearing them using a harpoon, a long pole with a barbed point at the end. Later, humans developed hooks made of materials such as bone, stone and wood to catch fish.

harpoon heads

Weapons 7 8

People used spears and axes to help them hunt animals. This cave painting shows hunters using the bow and arrow. First used 18,000 years ago, it allowed people to hunt from a distance.

Farming

The development of farming changed how people lived. Before farming, people had to move around to find food. However, farmers stayed in one place to harvest their crops.

1 When did farming first begin?

2 Where is Mesopotamia?

3 Which rivers fed the farms of Mesopotamia?

4 What type of plants are cereals?

5 Re-arrange ZEIAM to spell a type of cereal.

6 Houses in Skara Brae are made of what material?

7 Where is Skara Brae?

8 People kept sheep on Skara Brae. True or false?

The first farms   1 2 3

Farming began in Mesopotamia in the Middle East around 10,000 years ago, at the end of the Stone Age. This region was fed by the Tigris and Euphrates rivers, and was very fertile. The land would produce many crops. More food meant that more people could live in the same place. Farms began to grow into villages and towns.

harvesting wheat

herding cattle

Cereal crops ④ ⑤

Cereals are plants that belong to the grass family. People domesticated them from wild plants. One of the most widely used cereals was wheat, but barley, millet and maize were also grown.

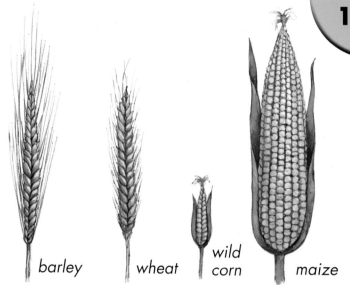

barley *wheat* *wild corn* *maize*

Skara Brae ⑥ ⑦ ⑧

Skara Brae is a prehistoric village built from stone. People lived there in the Stone Age. It is in the Orkney Islands, north of Scotland. The villagers lived off crops, sheep and cattle. They also ate fish.

farm building

goat

Metal work

After the Stone Age, people learned how to make things from metal. Bronze and iron were the first two metals people used to make objects.

1 Re-arrange ZEBNRO to spell a metal.

2 Where did the Bronze Age begin?

3 Bronze is made of which two metals?

4 Why was bronze used to make weapons?

5 Bronze was not used to make bracelets. True or false?

6 Why did people use iron instead of bronze?

7 Why is iron useful?

8 Name a weapon made of iron.

Bronze Age　　① ② ③

The Bronze Age began in Europe and Asia around 5,000 years ago. Bronze was made by melting copper and tin together. Bronze is hard and easy to work with. It could be made into many different objects, such as spears.

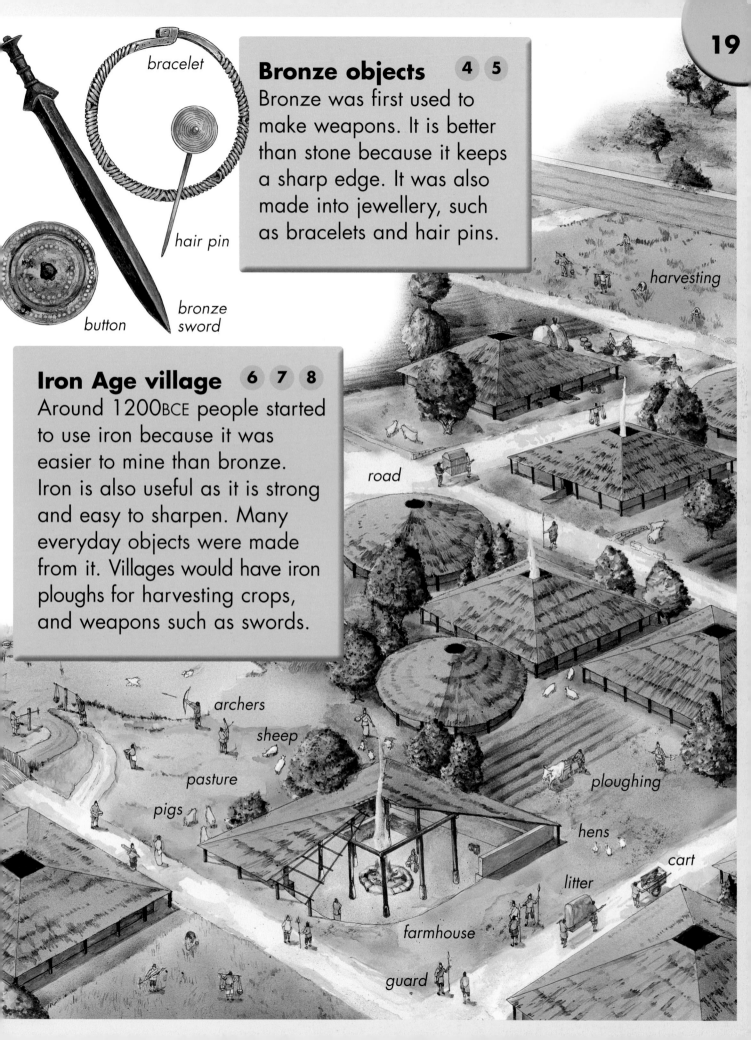

bracelet

hair pin

button

bronze
sword

Bronze objects 4 5

Bronze was first used to
make weapons. It is better
than stone because it keeps
a sharp edge. It was also
made into jewellery, such
as bracelets and hair pins.

harvesting

Iron Age village 6 7 8

Around 1200BCE people started
to use iron because it was
easier to mine than bronze.
Iron is also useful as it is strong
and easy to sharpen. Many
everyday objects were made
from it. Villages would have iron
ploughs for harvesting crops,
and weapons such as swords.

road

archers

sheep

pasture

pigs

ploughing

hens

cart

litter

farmhouse

guard

PREHISTORY
History makers

1. Humans and apes began to evolve in different ways between eight and five million years ago.

2. Fire was probably used for the first time by *Homo erectus*, in around 1,500,000BCE.

3. *Homo sapiens* are thought to have first arrived in Europe around 40,000BCE.

4. Neanderthals were closely related to humans. They died out around 30,000BCE.

5. The oldest known cave paintings date from 30,000BCE and are in France.

6. The oldest piece of pottery in the world is a small statue dating from around 25,000BCE.

7. The first bread was made around 10,000BCE.

8. The first wild animal to have been trained by *Homo sapiens* was the dog. They helped hunters and guarded settlements.

9. Until around 10,000BCE, large parts of the Earth were covered with ice.

10. *Homo sapiens* hunted the auroch. It was a huge wild ox that stood nearly 2 metres high.

Chapter two
ANCIENT WORLDS
5000BCE – 500CE

The Sumerians

About 7,000 years ago, the Sumerians created a great civilization in the Middle East that lasted 3,000 years. They built some of the first cities and invented many new things.

1 Which two rivers run through the fertile crescent?

2 Sumer lies in what modern country?

3 Ur was a large city. True or false?

4 What was at the centre of Ur?

5 What did the Sumerians write with?

6 What writing system did the Sumerians use?

7 Unjumble HWELE to spell a Sumerian invention.

8 What did the Sumerians first use the wheel for?

The fertile crescent

1 2

Sumer was in the southeast of an area called the fertile crescent, between the Tigris and Euphrates rivers. This land was later known as Mesopotamia (now Iraq). The soil was perfect for farming. When the rivers flooded, the land became wet and fertile. Crops grew well there.

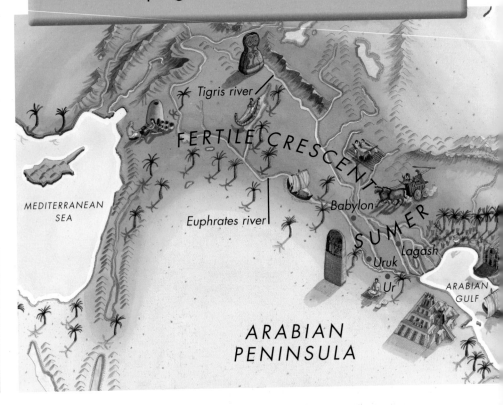

Tigris river

FERTILE CRESCENT

MEDITERRANEAN SEA

Euphrates river

Babylon

SUMER

Uruk

Lagash

Ur

ARABIAN GULF

ARABIAN PENINSULA

A great city 3 4

Ur was one of the first large cities in the world. At the centre of the city was the Great Ziggurat of Ur. This was a stepped pyramid that was used as a temple. The Ziggurat was built more than 4,000 years ago.

stylus

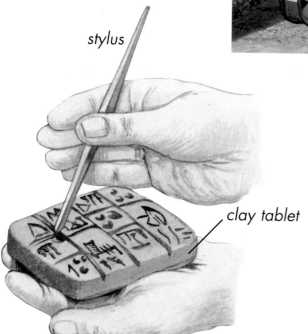

clay tablet

Inventing the wheel 7 8

The Sumerians are believed to have invented the wheel, one of history's most important inventions. At first, they used the wheel to shape pottery. Later they used it on carts.

Sumerian writing 5 6

The Sumerians wrote by making marks with a stylus, a sharpened piece of reed, onto slabs of damp clay, called tablets. This script is called cuneiform and was one of the world's first writing systems.

Pharaohs

Pharaoh was the title given to the kings of ancient Egypt. They were among the most powerful and important rulers of the ancient world.

1. Who was in charge of the army and government?

2. The pharaohs were believed to be gods. True or false?

3. Who uses a crook?

4. What is used to harvest grain?

5. What is the name of the falcon god?

6. How were bodies of dead pharaohs preserved?

7. What was removed from the pharaoh's body after he died?

8. Re-arrange HPSSUAAGOCR to spell a stone container.

A divine ruler

1 **2**

The pharaoh was in charge of the army and government. Most importantly, the pharaoh was at the heart of ancient Egyptian religion. He was worshipped as a god on Earth by his people.

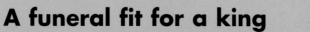

flail

crook

Regalia   3   4   5

Items called regalia were symbols of power worn by the pharaoh. The crook and flail showed people the pharaoh would protect and feed them. Shepherds used crooks to herd and control sheep, and flails were used to harvest grain. The pharaoh also wore symbols of the falcon-god Horus.

Horus

A funeral fit for a king   6   7   8

When a pharaoh died, his body was mummified to preserve it. First it was dried out with a kind of salt. Then the stomach, liver, lungs and intestines were removed. Then it was placed in a boat and taken in a procession to the royal tomb, inside a pyramid, where it was put into a stone container called a sarcophagus. The pyramid was then sealed to stop robbers.

brightly painted sarcophagus

Pyramid building

The pyramids were built more than 3,000 years ago as tombs for the pharaohs. For thousands of years they were the largest man-made structures.

1 How many pyramids are there at Giza?

2 The Great Pyramid took 200 years to build. True or false?

3 How many stone blocks are in the Great Pyramid?

4 How many craftsmen shaped the stone blocks?

5 What tools did the craftsmen use?

6 How were the blocks moved?

7 How many workers built a pyramid?

8 Unjumble SANOCTEP to spell a pyramid-shaped stone.

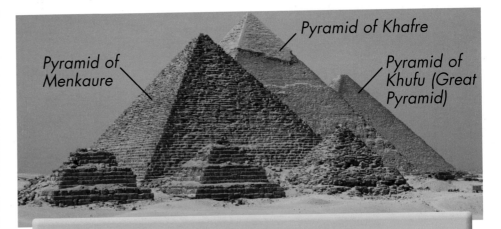

Pyramid of Khafre

Pyramid of Menkaure

Pyramid of Khufu (Great Pyramid)

Pyramids at Giza 1 2 3
There are three pyramids at Giza. The Great Pyramid was built for King Khufu to be buried in. It took 20 years to build and is made of over two million stone blocks.

Stonework 4 5
The pyramids were made of stone. Around 4,000 craftsmen shaped this into blocks using pickaxes, hammers and chisels.

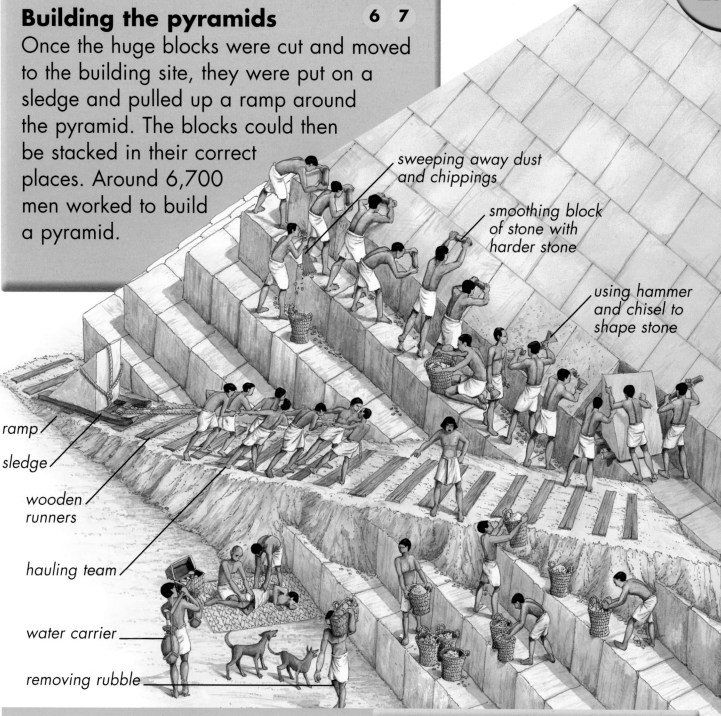

Building the pyramids **6** **7**

Once the huge blocks were cut and moved to the building site, they were put on a sledge and pulled up a ramp around the pyramid. The blocks could then be stacked in their correct places. Around 6,700 men worked to build a pyramid.

sweeping away dust and chippings

smoothing block of stone with harder stone

using hammer and chisel to shape stone

ramp

sledge

wooden runners

hauling team

water carrier

removing rubble

Finishing touch **8**

To complete the building, a pyramid-shaped stone was placed at the very top. This was called the 'capstone'. Sometimes this stone would be covered in gold.

Olympic Games

The Olympic Games were ancient Greek athletic contests. They were first held more than 2,700 years ago and inspired the modern Olympics, which began in 1896.

1 When did the Olympic Games probably begin?

2 How often were the Olympic Games?

3 Who was Zeus?

4 Olympia is in northeast Greece. True or false?

5 What was the statue of Zeus at Olympia made of?

6 What was the first event at the Olympic Games?

7 Unjumble CSIDSU to spell an event.

8 What was the woman-only event held at Olympia called?

The first games ① ② ③

The Olympic Games probably began in 776 BCE. They took place every four years as part of a religious festival held to honour Zeus, the king of the Greek gods.

wrestling

discus throwing

running

Olympia 4 5

The games were held in Olympia, in southwest Greece. In Olympia there was a magnificent statue of Zeus, made mostly from ivory and gold. There was also a large gymnasium (see right) where athletes trained. Olympia's buildings are now stone ruins.

chariot racing

long jump

The events 6 7

Sprinting was the first Olympic event. Later, the athletes ran longer races. Boxing, wrestling, chariot racing, long jump, javelin and discus were added to later games.

Women's Olympics 8

Women were usually not allowed to compete except in contests involving horses. However, they had a separate event in Olympia called the Heraean Games.

The Romans

The Romans were great builders and soldiers. From 27 BCE to 476 CE they ruled one of the largest empires of the ancient world.

1 What did most Romans wear every day?

2 What is a toga?

3 What did Roman soldiers wear?

4 Wealthy Romans bought slaves. True or false?

5 What was the centre of a town called?

6 Where did most Romans live?

7 Did wealthy Romans eat lying down at feasts?

8 Unjumble RMODOSEU to spell a favourite Roman food.

toga

Roman clothing ① ② ③

Most Romans wore a plain tunic for everyday life. On special occasions they wore togas. This was a cloth wrapped around the body. Roman soldiers wore metal armour and helmets.

soldier

Town life ④ ⑤ ⑥

A Market stalls selling a variety of fruit and vegetables.

B Slaves being bought by wealthy Romans.

C Hot food being prepared.

D A road leading to the centre of town. The centre of town was called the forum. It was used as a meeting place.

E Most people lived in apartment blocks known as *insulae*.

F A wealthy Roman's garden.

G Shop selling cloth.

A

Roman feasts

Wealthy Romans enjoyed having parties. They ate lying down on couches. Slaves brought them food and drink. One of their favourite foods was the dormouse. Musicians and dancers performed while the guests ate.

The ancient Chinese

The ancient Chinese era lasted from 1600 to 221 BCE. They are famous for their important inventions, the Great Wall and artistic creations.

1 Why was the Great Wall built?

2 When did building start on the Wall?

3 What was the Great Wall's total length?

4 Re-arrange PERPA to spell a Chinese invention.

5 How was the wheelbarrow used?

6 Terracotta is a type of clay. True or false?

7 What did most ancient Chinese peasants work as?

8 Where did peasants sell their produce?

The Great Wall of China 1 2 3

The Great Wall was built to defend China from attack. Building started in the 5th century BCE, and the Wall helped protect China for about 2,000 years. When it was finished it was about 8,850km long.

brick top

stone wall

bricks and paving blocks

rubble

Inventions 4 5

The four greatest inventions were the compass, gunpowder, paper and printing. The ancient Chinese also invented a wheelbarrow that could carry heavy weights.

wheelbarrow

Terracotta 6

The ancient Chinese made sculptures out of a clay called terracotta. Terracotta was used in 210BCE to make a life-sized army to guard the emperor Qin Shi Huangdi's tomb.

watch tower

terracotta army

stone quarry

scaffolding

Daily life 7 8

Most people were peasants, who mainly worked as farmers. They grew crops such as rice and raised pigs. Peasants would sell their produce at town markets.

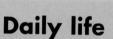

The Mayans

The Maya people were a civilization located in Central America. From 2000BCE the Mayans built many large cities and monuments, and also used a very advanced writing system.

1 Mayan pyramids have steps. True or false?

2 What was at the top of many Mayan pyramids?

3 What colour was Chichén Itzá?

4 What was the ball game called?

5 How many teams played in the Mayan ball game?

6 Unjumble UBRBRE to spell a material.

7 Who was the most important Mayan god?

8 Did the Mayans make human sacrifices?

Step pyramids 1 2

The Maya built huge pyramids including this one at Chichén Itzá. The pyramids were made of layers of stone built into steps, then painted and covered with carvings. Many pyramids had a temple or an observatory at the top.

3 *red paint*

carving

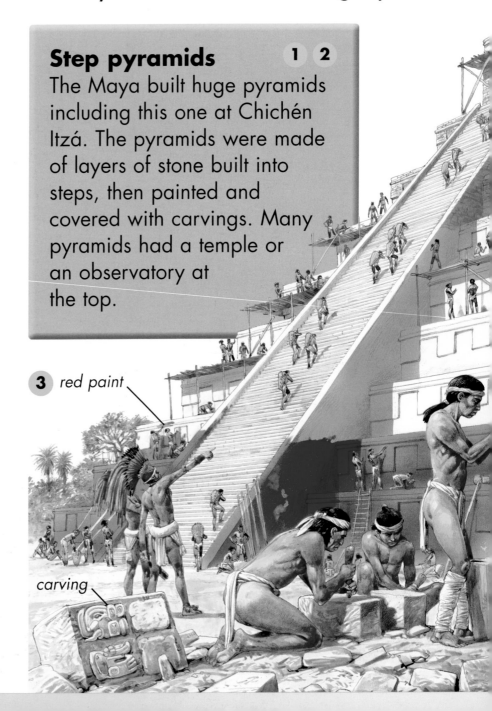

Pok-a-tok   4 5 6

In this ball game, two teams had to keep a rubber ball in play using only their elbows, hips and thighs. The aim was to hit the ball through a stone ring.

stone ring

Religion   7 8

The Mayans worshipped many gods. Itzamna was the most important god. They believed he had created the world. They made offerings to their gods – sometimes even human sacrifices.

temple

steps

loin cloth

basket

The Celts

The Celts were a group of tribes that had, by 275 BCE, spread across Europe. These tribes often went to war against the Romans and one another.

1. What were Celtic houses called?

2. What shape were the roofs?

3. Where in the house was the fire?

4. Where did the Celts place their forts?

5. Re-arrange CDSTIHE to spell something the Celts built for protection.

6. The Celts had many gods. True or false?

7. What were the Celts' main weapons?

8. What colour did warriors in Britain paint themselves?

Celtic houses

1 2 3

The Celts lived in circular dwellings called roundhouses. These had cone-shaped thatched roofs made of straw. In the middle of the house there was a fire for heat, light and cooking. Celtic houses did not have any windows.

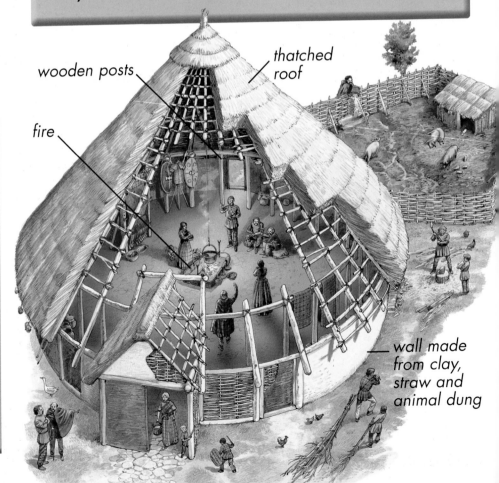

wooden posts

thatched roof

fire

wall made from clay, straw and animal dung

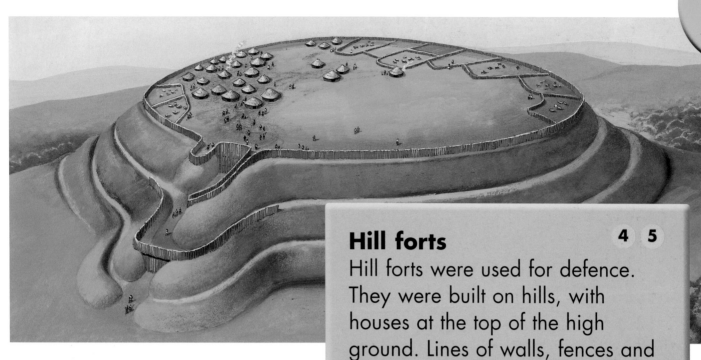

Hill forts 4 5

Hill forts were used for defence. They were built on hills, with houses at the top of the high ground. Lines of walls, fences and ditches were built to protect the people inside from attackers.

Beliefs 6

The Celts were polytheists, which means they worshipped many different gods. One was Cernunnos, who was shown with antlers (above). The Celts built temples and shrines. In some places there were groups of people called druids, who acted as priests.

The Celts at war 7 8

The Celts' main weapons were the sword and shield. Before fighting, warriors often painted their skin. In Britain, they used a plant called woad to paint themselves blue.

bronze shield

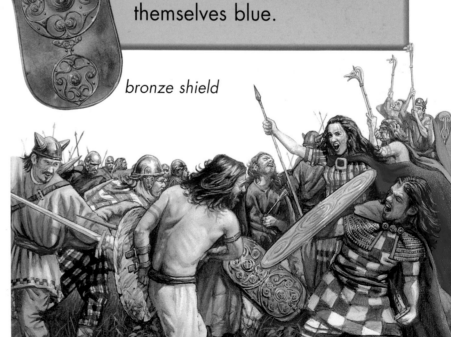

ANCIENT WORLDS
History makers

1. The largest of the three pyramids at Giza is the Great Pyramid. Today it is nearly 140 metres tall.

2. The poet Homer wrote the *Odyssey* near the end of the 8th century BCE. It is still read today.

3. The Hanging Gardens of Babylon are believed to have been built around 600BCE.

4. By the time of his death in 323BCE, Alexander the Great had conquered all of Egypt and Persia.

5. The Colossus of Rhodes was a giant statue of the Greek sun god Helios. It was finished in 280BCE.

6. The first ruler of a united China was Qin Shi Huangdi. He was emperor from 221 to 210BCE.

7. The Circus Maximus in Rome was used to hold chariot races. It could seat 250,000 people.

8. The longest reign of an emperor of ancient China was by Wu of Han. He ruled from 141 to 87BCE.

9. The first Roman emperor was called Gaius Octavius Augustus. He ruled from 31BCE to 14CE.

10. The Mayans were interested in the planets. They believed Venus was associated with war.

Chapter three
THE MIDDLE AGES
500CE – 1450CE

The Vikings

The Vikings came from Scandinavia in northern Europe. From the late 700s until the 1060s, Viking warriors raided the coasts of Europe. They were also skilled explorers and traders.

1 Viking warriors used war axes. True or false?

2 What did rich Vikings wear in battle?

3 What is chainmail?

4 Where did they set up trade routes?

5 Re-arrange OYEHN to spell an item Vikings traded.

6 What were Viking boats called?

7 Which two large islands did the Vikings discover?

8 What did the Vikings call North America?

Viking warriors   ① ② ③

The Vikings were feared fighters. Warriors went into battle carrying spears, shields and war axes. Rich Vikings wore helmets and chainmail. Chainmail is a type of armour made of small, linked metal rings.

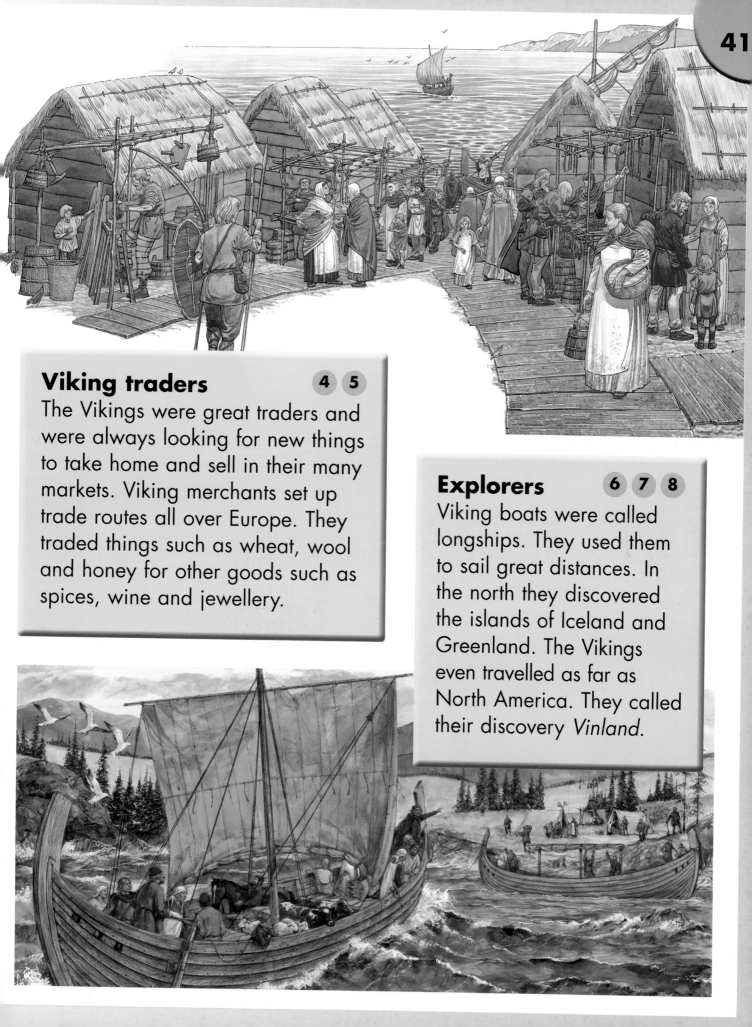

Viking traders 4 5

The Vikings were great traders and were always looking for new things to take home and sell in their many markets. Viking merchants set up trade routes all over Europe. They traded things such as wheat, wool and honey for other goods such as spices, wine and jewellery.

Explorers 6 7 8

Viking boats were called longships. They used them to sail great distances. In the north they discovered the islands of Iceland and Greenland. The Vikings even travelled as far as North America. They called their discovery *Vinland*.

The Normans

In 1066 the Normans, from northern France, invaded England. They were led by William, who defeated the English at the Battle of Hastings. William became king of England.

1 When was the Battle of Hastings?

2 The English fought on horses. True or false?

3 What was the name of the English king killed at Hastings?

4 What is the Bayeux Tapestry made of?

5 How long is the Bayeux Tapestry?

6 What type of castle did the Normans build in England?

7 What was the tower on top of the motte called?

8 Re-arrange LBIEYA to spell the fenced area of a castle.

Battle of Hastings ① ② ③

The Battle of Hastings took place on 14 October 1066. The Normans rode horses and the English fought on foot. Both sides used bows, shields, spears, axes and swords. Late in the battle the English king, Harold, was killed, probably by an arrow.

Norman knights

Bayeux Tapestry (4)(5)

The Bayeux Tapestry is made of cloth and decorated using a needle and thread. It is nearly 70 metres long and tells the story of the Norman conquest of England.

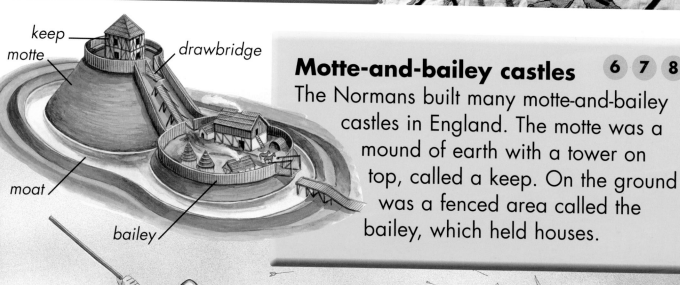

keep

motte

drawbridge

moat

bailey

Motte-and-bailey castles (6)(7)(8)

The Normans built many motte-and-bailey castles in England. The motte was a mound of earth with a tower on top, called a keep. On the ground was a fenced area called the bailey, which held houses.

English soldiers

Castles

By the 1100s, most castles were no longer built from wood. Instead, European nobles began to build much stronger ones made out of stone.

1 What was the most common type of castle?

2 What made a keep harder to attack?

3 Why were towers added to castles?

4 What would defenders shoot from high walls?

5 Cold oil was tipped onto attackers. True or false?

6 Re-arrange RLASO to spell the name of a castle room.

7 What part of the castle did the lord and lady live in?

8 Who lived at the top of the tower?

The castle

1 **2** **3**

There were many different types of castle. The most common was a simple square stone tower, called a keep. To make this harder to attack, walls would be built around it. Gatehouses and towers were also added for defence.

keep

round tower

outer wall

outer bailey

Castle defences   4 5

Capturing a medieval castle was not easy. The defenders shot arrows from the high walls. They also threw stones and poured cauldrons of boiling hot oil onto attacking soldiers through openings in the walls.

inner wall

inner bailey

gatehouse

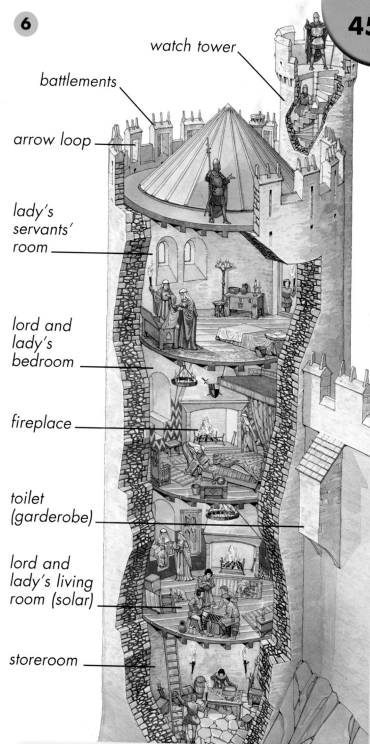

watch tower

battlements

arrow loop

lady's servants' room

lord and lady's bedroom

fireplace

toilet (garderobe)

lord and lady's living room (solar)

storeroom

Living in a castle   7 8

The lord and lady of the castle lived in the main tower. They had their own bedroom and comfortable living room. The lady's servants lived in the highest room in the tower.

The Black Death

The Black Death was a deadly plague that appeared about 1346. The disease started in Asia and spread into Europe and Africa. It lasted many years and killed millions of people.

1 What probably caused the Black Death?

2 Unjumble ELFA to spell an insect.

3 How did humans become infected with the plague?

4 How did people try to stop it from spreading?

5 What were the dead buried in?

6 Where did the Black Death spread quickly?

7 Towns had modern toilets. True or false?

8 Where did people throw their waste?

Rats and fleas   1 2 3

The cause of the Black Death was probably a disease called bubonic plague. Tiny insects called fleas carried the bacteria that caused the plague. Fleas lived on the rats and mice that infested towns. Humans caught the plague from flea bites.

flea

black rat

Fighting the Black Death   4

People tried to stop the plague spreading. Watchmen would guard the gates of towns and cities to stop outsiders entering. This is called quarantine.

watchman

Collecting the dead 5

Men were hired to collect the dead. They pulled carts through the streets. The bodies were buried away from towns and villages to try and stop the disease spreading. Bodies were often buried together in large holes called plague pits.

waste being thrown out of a window

Unclean cities 6 7 8

The Black Death spread very quickly in towns. This is because they were usually filthy and full of rats. The houses were very close together. This meant the plague could spread easily. There were no modern toilets. Instead, people threw their waste onto the street.

dead body

open sewer

The Incas

The Incas were from South America. During the 1400s they created a large empire. The Incas built their cities high in the Andes mountains. They were eventually conquered by the Spanish in the 16th century.

1 What decorated Inca headdresses?

2 Only Inca women wore jewellery. True or false?

3 What was the sun god called?

4 Re-arrange AAMM LAIQUL to spell out the name of the Inca moon goddess.

5 What was the ceremonial knife called?

6 What were houses made from?

7 What country is Machu Picchu in?

8 When was Machu Picchu built?

Inca clothing

Inca nobles wore brightly coloured tunics made from fine materials. They also wore headdresses decorated with feathers. Both noble men and women wore lots of jewellery. Ordinary people wore clothes made of cheap material.

headdress

jewellery

tunic made from fine material

Inca Gods ③ ④ ⑤

There were many Inca gods. The two most important were Inti, the sun god, and Mama Quilla, the moon goddess. The Incas often made animal sacrifices to them. They would use a ceremonial knife called the *tumi*.

ceremonial knife

Inca builders ⑥

The Incas were great builders and constructed large towns. Their houses were made from stone with thatched roofs. They also built excellent roads that linked their cities together. The Incas were skilled farmers and created terraces of flat ground in the mountains to grow crops on.

Machu Picchu ⑦ ⑧

Machu Picchu is a ruined but well-preserved Inca settlement. It is in the Andes mountains in Peru. It was built for an Inca emperor in the 15th century.

The samurai

The samurai were elite warriors from Japan. They were highly skilled and loyal soldiers. Samurai served both the Japanese emperor and various local lords until the 19th century.

1 What was the most important weapon?

2 Re-arrange ZSKWAAIIH to spell out the name of a samurai weapon.

3 The *naginata* is a short, blunt pole. True or false?

4 How were samurai meant to be towards their masters?

5 What does *Bushido* mean?

6 What did samurai wear to protect themselves in battle?

7 What was samurai armour made of?

8 What decorated samurai helmets?

Samurai weapons   1 2 3

The most important samurai weapon was a long, curved sword called the *katana*. They would also carry a dagger called a *wakizashi*. The samurai used many other weapons, too, including bows and arrows, clubs and the *naginata*, a long pole topped with a curved blade.

Samurai battledress 6 7 8

Samurai wore armour to protect themselves. It was made from pieces of leather and iron, joined together. This armour was strong and flexible. Samurai wore iron helmets to protect their head and necks. These helmets were sometimes decorated with antlers.

Way of life 4 5

The samurai were supposed to lead honourable lives. They were meant to be obedient and loyal to their masters until death. This code is called *Bushido*, which means 'the way of the warrior'.

bow

helmet

arrows in a quiver

leather and iron armour

bronze armour

mounted samurai

spear

samurai soldier

naginata

katana

THE MIDDLE AGES
History makers

1. The first recorded female emperor of Japan was Suiko. She ruled for over thirty years until her death in 628.

2. Charlemagne was king of the Franks from 768 to 814. He ruled over most of Western Europe.

3. The Viking invasion of England was stopped by the Saxons at the Battle of Edington in 878.

4. In 1001 the Viking explorer Leif Ericson became the first European to land on mainland America.

5. William the Conqueror ordered a survey of England, called the Domesday Book. It was completed in 1086.

6. Between 1095 and 1291 Christians in Europe fought to capture the city of Jerusalem. This period is known as the Crusades.

7. The longbow was a powerful weapon. It could fire arrows over 200 metres and pierce a knight's armour.

8. Between 1347 and 1351, around 25 million people died in Europe as a result of the Black Death.

9. Joan of Arc was a peasant girl who led the French army against the English. She was captured and executed in 1431.

10. In 1438 the Inca empire expanded rapidly. They were led by Pachacuti, whose name means 'earth shaker'.

Chapter four
EXPLORATION AND EMPIRES
1450 – 1900

Explorers

1 Who paid for Columbus's voyage?

2 On what date did Columbus land in the Bahamas?

3 What does *conquistadors* mean?

4 Who attacked the Aztec empire?

5 Re-arrange ALMGNLEA to spell an explorer's name.

6 Where was Magellan killed?

7 What was the name of da Gama's ship?

8 Da Gama sailed around America. True or false?

From the 15th to the 17th century, European explorers sailed across the world. They discovered America and other new lands. This period is called the Age of Discovery.

Christopher Columbus ① ②

In 1492, Christopher Columbus led a voyage across the Atlantic Ocean. It was paid for by Queen Isabella of Spain. The first land they spotted was the Bahamas in the Caribbean. They landed there on 12 October. Columbus did not know he was in the Americas – he thought he was in Asia!

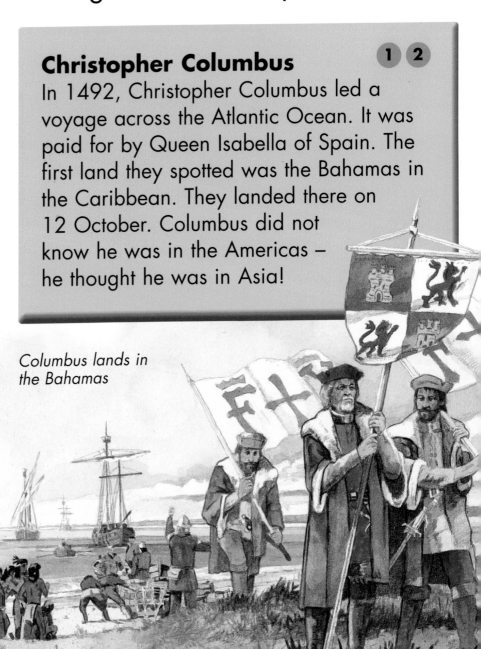

Columbus lands in the Bahamas

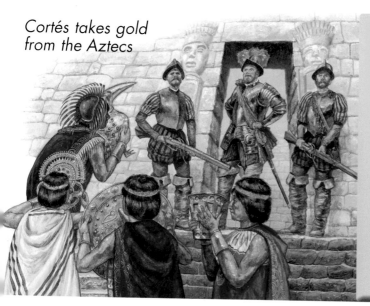

Cortés takes gold from the Aztecs

The conquistadors 3 4

Following Columbus's voyages, many Spanish explorers and soldiers travelled to the Americas. They were called *conquistadors*, which means 'conquerors'. In 1519 Hernán Cortés attacked the Aztec empire in Mexico. He defeated them in 1521 and took their gold.

Around the world 5 6

Ferdinand Magellan was the leader of the first expedition that sailed around the world. However, Magellan did not survive the voyage. In 1521 he was killed in the Philippines.

Magellan

Vasco da Gama 7 8

In 1497, Vasco da Gama led the first voyage from Europe to India. In his ship, the *São Gabriel*, he sailed around Africa and into the Indian Ocean. He faced huge storms before landing in India.

the São Gabriel

Pirates

Pirates were bands of criminals who sailed the seas robbing ships. Between the 1650s and the 1720s, pirates attacked ships in the Caribbean.

1 What ships did pirates attack?

2 What was Edward Teach known as?

3 Who got the biggest share of the loot?

4 Rich prisoners were held for ransom. True or false?

5 Re-arrange YLJLO OREGR to spell the name of the flag pirate ships flew.

6 What was the most famous design of a pirate flag?

7 Which captain buried his treasure?

8 Where was Kidd's treasure buried?

Pirate attack! ① ②

Pirates attacked merchant ships carrying expensive goods. Led by captains such as Edward Teach, known as 'Blackbeard', they would sail towards a ship and leap onto its deck to capture it. Pirates used all sorts of weapons.

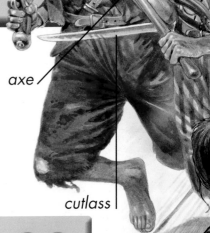

axe

cutlass

musket

After the raid ③ ④

After pirates captured a ship, they divided the cargo among themselves. The captain got the largest share. Rich prisoners were often held for ransom.

PIRATE CAPTAINS AND THEIR FLAGS

Black Bart

Christopher Moody

Blackbeard

Henry Every

Calico Jack

Thomas Tew

Blackbeard

pistol

Pirate flags 5 6

Pirate ships would fly special flags called Jolly Rogers to scare the ships they attacked. The most famous design was a white skull and cross-bones on a black background. Many captains had their own flags.

Captain Kidd

Buried treasure 7 8

A popular story about pirates is that they buried their treasure. The only captain who definitely did this was William Kidd. He buried some of his plunder on Gardiners Island, near New York, in the late 17th century.

Slavery

lavery has existed since ancient times. It reached its peak in the 18th and 19th centuries. Slaves are the property of their master. They must work without being paid and can be sold to someone else.

1 Where were most slaves taken from?

2 What ocean did many slaves cross?

3 Where in Africa did Arab slave traders work?

4 Unjumble LDGO to spell a trade item.

5 Where did the Arab traders sell their slaves?

6 What was cotton used to make?

7 Abolitionists wanted to end slavery. True or false?

8 What year was slavery ended in the United States?

The Atlantic slave trade 1 2
From the 16th to the 19th century, slave traders captured millions of African men, women and children. Most slaves were taken from the west coast of Africa. They were chained together and put on slave ships. These vessels carried them across the Atlantic Ocean to be sold in the Americas.

Arab slave market

Arab traders 3 4 5

Arab slave traders had existed in Africa from around 650. They worked mainly in East Africa. People were captured and traded for cloth, jewellery, pottery and gold. The slaves were then sold in the Middle East and North Africa.

sugar cane plantation

Plantations 6

Plantations were large farms that grew crops. Slaves were often used to do all the work. Conditions were normally bad and the work was hard. Slaves grew important crops such as sugar cane and coffee. In the southern United States the main plantation crop was cotton. It was used to make cloth.

Ending slavery 7 8

Many people wanted to end slavery. They were known as 'abolitionists'. One abolitionist was Frederick Douglass (right). He had escaped slavery and wanted it stopped. The United States ended slavery in 1865.

cotton plant

Kings and queens

Between the 16th and 18th centuries, the kings and queens of Europe held large amounts of power. They had total control over their subjects.

1 How many wives did Henry VIII have?

2 Who was Henry VIII's first wife?

3 What was Elizabeth I also known as?

4 What year was the Spanish Armada defeated?

5 Re-arrange YAMR UATRST to spell the name of William of Orange's wife.

6 When did William arrive in England?

7 What year was the Battle of the Boyne?

8 Louis XVI was executed in 1693. True or false?

Henry VIII

1 2

From 1509 to 1547, Henry VIII was king of England. He is remembered for having six wives. Henry was also responsible for splitting England from the Catholic Church. The split happened because the pope would not let him divorce his first wife, Catherine of Aragon. Henry married his second wife, Anne Boleyn, in 1533.

Henry VIII and Anne Boleyn

William of Orange at the Battle of the Boyne

Elizabeth I ③ ④

Elizabeth I was the second daughter of Henry VIII. She was queen of England between 1558 and 1603. Elizabeth never married, and was called 'The Virgin Queen'. The most important event of her reign was the defeat of the Spanish Armada in 1588 – this was an invasion fleet of ships.

William of Orange ⑤ ⑥ ⑦

William of Orange, a Dutch prince, married Mary Stuart, the daughter of James II, the king of England. In 1689 William arrived in England and tried to take power. This led to war, and in 1690 William defeated James at the Battle of the Boyne.

Louis XVI ⑧

In France the king was very powerful. Louis XVI was the French king from 1774 to 1792. Louis was not a good leader. He became so unpopular that his people rebelled. The government executed Louis in 1793.

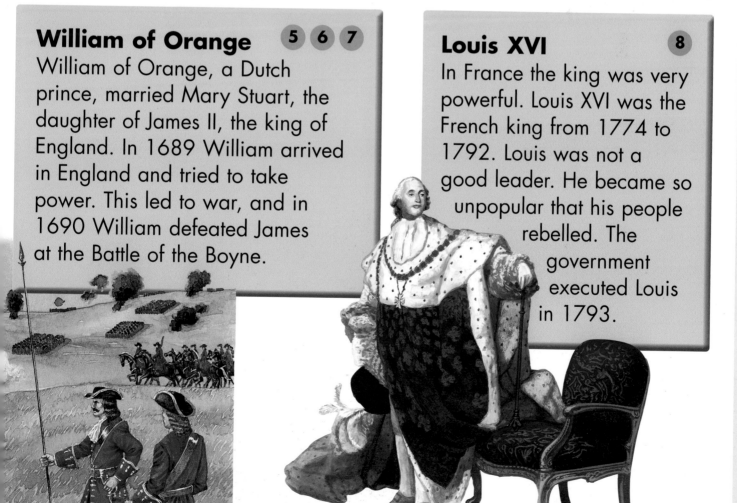

Age of Revolution

Revolutions attempt to change how a country is ruled. In the late 18th and early 19th centuries, many took place across the world. Often, kings were replaced by governments chosen by the people.

1 There were 14 American colonies. True or false?

2 Which empire did the colonies fight?

3 What country did the colonies form?

4 What year did the French Revolution start?

5 Who ruled France after Louis XVI?

6 Unjumble LUETNOLGII to spell a device.

7 Who was Simón Bolívar?

8 By what date had most of South America won independence?

American revolution

1 2 3

In the 18th century there were 13 colonies in America. These were part of the British empire. Americans became unhappy with British rule and a war started in 1775. The colonies joined together to become the United States of America. They defeated Britain in 1781 and became independent.

British soldiers surrender to the Americans

French revolution ④ ⑤

A revolution began in France in 1789. The people were angry as there was little food and high taxes. In 1792, the king, Louis XVI, was replaced as ruler by the National Convention. This was elected by men over the age of 25 and it ruled for three years.

French revolutionaries build a barricade

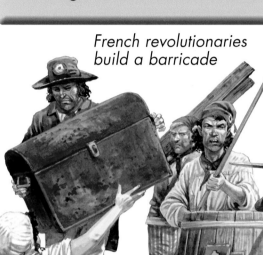

guillotine

Guillotine ⑥

During the French Revolution thousands of people were killed by the guillotine. This was a sharp blade that chopped off people's heads.

Simón Bolívar ⑦ ⑧

Most of South America was controlled by Spain. In the early 1800s, people rose up and fought to end Spanish rule. The most important revolutionary leader was Simón Bolívar. He helped most of South America become independent by 1829.

Spanish soldiers

Simón Bolívar

The Napoleonic Wars

The Napoleonic Wars were a series of conflicts that started in 1803 and ended in 1815. France was led by general Napoleon Bonaparte. He fought all of the major European powers and won many victories.

1 Where was Napoleon born?

2 What year did he become emperor?

3 What was Napoleon's most famous victory?

4 Napoleon invaded Britain. True or false?

5 What country did France invade in 1812?

6 In what year did Napoleon fight his last battle?

7 Where did this battle take place?

8 Unjumble APISURS to spell a country at the battle.

Napoleon leads his troops to victory

The rise of Napoleon 1 2

Napoleon Bonaparte was born on Corsica in 1769, and became an officer in the French army. After the French Revolution, his fame grew quickly thanks to his many successes in battle. Napoleon eventually became the leader of France in 1799, and in 1804 he became emperor.

War in Europe ③ ④

In 1805 Napoleon won his most famous victory, at the Battle of Austerlitz. He destroyed both an Austrian and a Russian army. However, in the same year, the French were beaten by the British navy at Trafalgar. This stopped Napoleon invading Britain and led to another ten years of war.

Invading Russia ⑤

France invaded Russia in June 1812. However, they could not beat the Russians. The French faced cold weather and attacks from Russian soldiers. Napoleon retreated. He had lost well over half of his men.

Russians attack the retreating French

Scottish soldiers

French cavalry

Battle of Waterloo ⑥ ⑦ ⑧

In June 1815, Napoleon lost his last battle against an alliance of European countries led by Prussia and Britain. The battle took place in modern-day Belgium, at a place called Waterloo. Napoleon was exiled and died in 1821.

Industrial Revolution

The Industrial Revolution started in Britain in the 18th century. New inventions transformed how people lived and worked. These changes soon spread across Europe and to the United States.

1 Who invented the spinning jenny?

2 What did Richard Arkwright invent?

3 What was at the centre of towns?

4 Where did the workers live?

5 Why were canals built?

6 Young children often had to work in factories. True or false?

7 Unjumble ESMAT to spell a type of power.

8 When did Robert Stephenson build the *Rocket*?

New inventions **1 2**

New machines changed how things were made. They allowed fewer workers to make more objects. Two new inventions increased the production of cloth. One was the spinning jenny, invented by James Hargreaves in 1764. The other was Richard Arkwright's spinning frame.

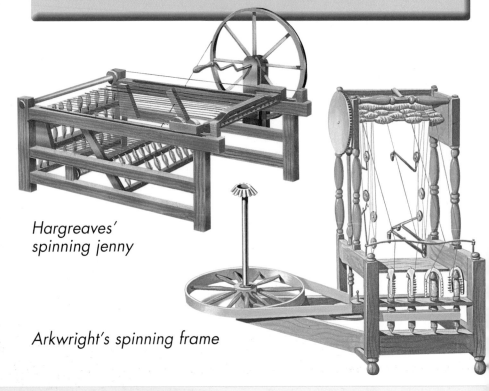

Hargreaves' spinning jenny

Arkwright's spinning frame

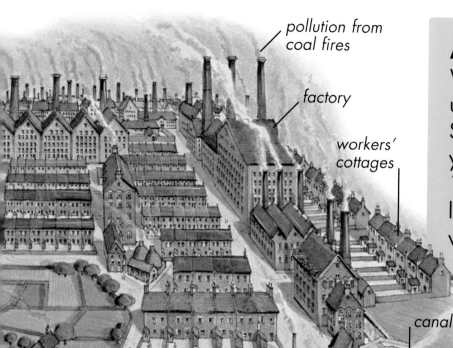

pollution from coal fires

factory

workers' cottages

canal

barge in a canal lock

At work **6**

Working in a factory was unpleasant and dangerous. Some employed children as young as four. During the 19th and 20th centuries, laws were made to improve working conditions.

worker in a factory

Factory towns **3** **4** **5**

At the centre of a town was the factory. As factories got bigger, so did the towns. The workers lived in cottages close by. Canals were built so boats could transport goods easily.

Steam power **7** **8**

Steam replaced older forms of power, such as horses. Water would be boiled by burning coal, creating jets of steam that pushed machinery, such as trains. In 1829 Robert Stephenson built the *Rocket*, an early steam-powered train.

smoke stack

water barrel

boiler

furnace

piston

Expanding empires

In the 19th century a number of European countries established empires in Africa and Asia. By far the largest empires were those of Britain and France.

1 In what century did Europeans rush to control Africa?

2 Belgium owned land in Africa. True or false?

3 Unjumble CIAVIROT to spell a British queen.

4 What was the largest empire?

5 Where was David Livingstone from?

6 In what year did Livingstone see the Victoria Falls?

7 In which continent was most of the French empire?

8 What was the Foreign Legion?

The scramble for Africa ①②

In the late 19th century, European countries rushed to gain control of Africa. By 1900, nations such as Belgium, France, Germany and Britain ruled nearly all of the continent. This was called 'the scramble for Africa'.

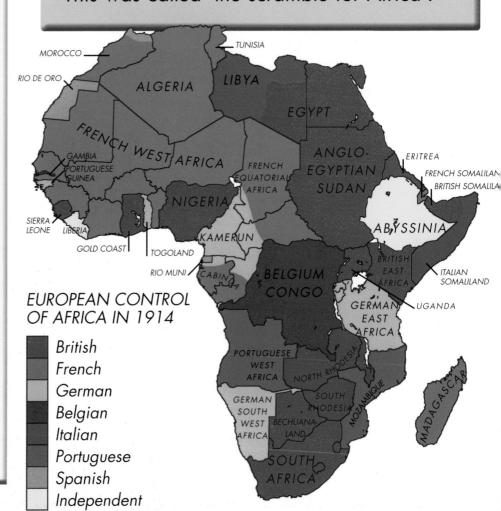

EUROPEAN CONTROL OF AFRICA IN 1914

British
French
German
Belgian
Italian
Portuguese
Spanish
Independent

MOROCCO
TUNISIA
RIO DE ORO
ALGERIA
LIBYA
EGYPT
FRENCH WEST AFRICA
GAMBIA
PORTUGUESE GUINEA
FRENCH EQUATORIAL AFRICA
ANGLO-EGYPTIAN SUDAN
ERITREA
FRENCH SOMALILAND
BRITISH SOMALILAND
NIGERIA
SIERRA LEONE
LIBERIA
GOLD COAST
TOGOLAND
KAMERUN
ABYSSINIA
RIO MUNI
CABINDA
BELGIUM CONGO
BRITISH EAST AFRICA
ITALIAN SOMALILAND
GERMAN EAST AFRICA
UGANDA
PORTUGUESE WEST AFRICA
NORTH RHODESIA
MOZAMBIQUE
MADAGASCAR
GERMAN SOUTH WEST AFRICA
SOUTH RHODESIA
BECHUANA LAND
SOUTH AFRICA

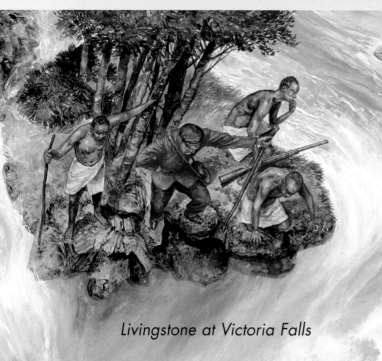

Livingstone at Victoria Falls

Exploring Africa 5 6

Before the 19th century, most of Africa was unknown to Europeans. Men such as David Livingstone, from Scotland, began to explore the continent. He was the first European to see the Victoria Falls, in 1855.

The British empire 3 4

Queen Victoria reigned from 1837 to 1901. During this time the British empire became the largest in history. By the early 1900s it covered a quarter of the world. Britain owned land on all of the continents.

The French conquest of Mali in West Africa

The French empire 7 8

France controlled a large empire, with territory in Asia, South America and Oceania. Most of France's empire was in Africa. To help defend this territory, France used an army unit called the Foreign Legion. Men from any country could join the Foreign Legion.

EXPLORATION AND EMPIRE
History makers

1. Only 55 of Vasco da Gama's crew of 170 people survived his first voyage to Asia in 1497 to 1498.

2. The first permanent English settlement in North America was Jamestown, in modern-day Virginia. It was founded in 1607.

3. Louis XIV became king of France in 1643, at only four years old. He ruled for 72 years until his death in 1715.

4. Although Henry Morgan was a famous pirate, King Charles II of England knighted him in 1674.

5. The first European explorer to reach New Zealand was Abel Tasman in 1642. However, no Europeans returned until James Cook's voyage in 1769.

6. Between 1789 and 1797 George Washington served as the first president of the United States.

7. During the French Revolution, between 16,000 and 40,000 people were executed by the guillotine.

8. Napoleon was made a general at the age of 24 in 1793.

9. The American Civil War took place between 1861 and 1865. It led to the end of slavery in the United States.

10. In 1876 Queen Victoria also became the Empress of India, which was part of the British empire.

Chapter five
THE MODERN WORLD
1900 – Today

First flight

People have tried to fly for centuries. Early attempts used gliders and balloons. In the 20th century, the first powered flights were made.

da Vinci's hang glider

Early attempts at flight   1 2

In the 11th century, a monk, Eilmer of Malmesbury, flew a short distance in a glider. Leonardo da Vinci drew plans for both a hang glider and a helicopter.

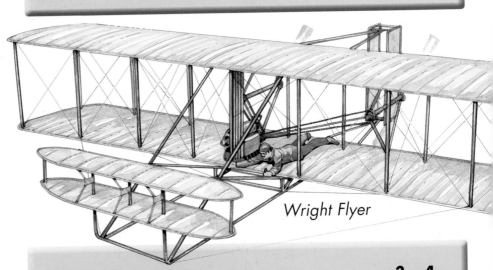

Wright Flyer

The Wright brothers   3 4

Orville and Wilbur Wright were American brothers and inventors. In 1903 they made the first ever powered flight. Orville flew their aeroplane for just 12 seconds.

1 What was the name of the monk who flew a glider?

2 What did da Vinci draw plans of?

3 Who made the first powered flight?

4 When was the first powered flight made?

5 Unjumble PMNOONLAE to spell an aeroplane.

6 When did Blériot cross the Channel?

7 Who created the first airship?

8 Aeroplanes were used in World War I. True or false?

Louis Blériot 5 6

In 1907, Louis Blériot was the first man to make a working aeroplane with one set of wings. This is called a monoplane. Two years later, in 1909, he flew his fourth design, the Blériot XI, across the English Channel. The journey took him 36 minutes.

Blériot XI monoplane

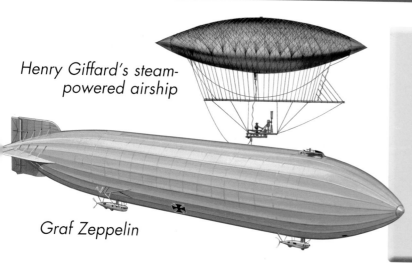
Henry Giffard's steam-powered airship

Graf Zeppelin

Airships 7

In 1852, Henri Giffard created the first airship by adding a steam-powered engine to a balloon. In the 20th century, larger airships, like the Graf Zeppelin, were developed.

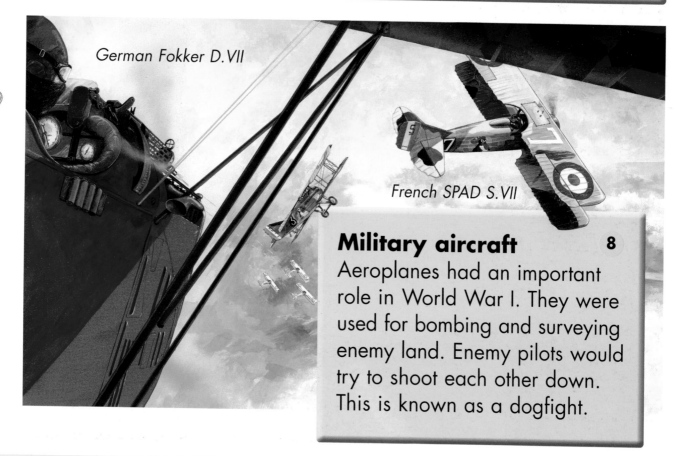
German Fokker D.VII

French SPAD S.VII

Military aircraft 8

Aeroplanes had an important role in World War I. They were used for bombing and surveying enemy land. Enemy pilots would try to shoot each other down. This is known as a dogfight.

Submarines

Submarines are vessels capable of travelling underwater. Some can travel long distances while underwater. Since World War I, submarines have mostly been used in warfare. They have also been used to explore deep oceans.

1 How were the first submarines powered?

2 Unjumble GMRESARU to spell an early submarine.

3 What powers the largest submarines?

4 What was the name of the first nuclear submarine?

5 Submersibles are very large. True or false?

6 Can submersibles be remote controlled?

7 What is a bathyscaphe?

8 How deep did the *Trieste* dive?

Early submarines   1   2

While there were a number of earlier efforts, the first working submarines were built in the 19th century. The first designs used hand-powered propellers. An early mechanical submarine was the *Resurgam*. This used steam power and was launched in 1879. It sank after less than a year. By the 20th century, submarines ran on diesel.

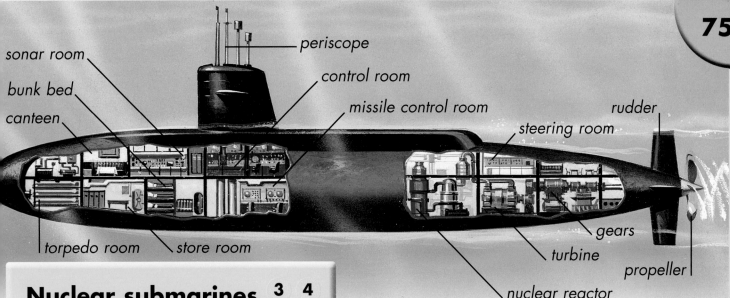

sonar room

bunk bed

canteen

periscope

control room

missile control room

rudder

steering room

torpedo room

store room

gears

turbine

propeller

nuclear reactor

Nuclear submarines 3 4

From the 1950s, the largest and most powerful submarines became nuclear powered. They can spend months underwater because they do not need to be refuelled very often. The first nuclear submarine was the American USS *Nautilus*.

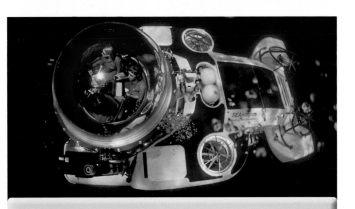

Submersibles 5 6

Very small underwater vessels are called submersibles. They cannot travel as far as submarines. Submersibles often have single-person crews, or are remote controlled.

Deep-sea exploration 7 8

A bathyscaphe is a vessel that can dive deep under the sea. In 1960, the *Trieste* went the deepest distance humans have ever been. It dove to a depth of more than 10,000 metres in the Mariana Trench, the Earth's deepest point. This is in the Pacific Ocean near Japan.

Films and TV

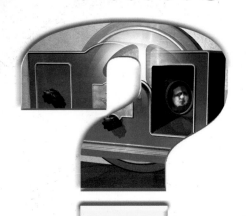

Cinema and television were developed and improved throughout the 20th century. They became the most popular forms of entertainment.

1 Before the 1920s films had sound. True or false?

2 Unjumble EHCRIAL LNIPCAH to spell an actor's name.

3 What was used to capture movement?

4 What material was used to make films?

5 In what year did Baird first televise moving objects?

6 What was projected onto a spinning disc?

7 Did Farnsworth's television use moving parts?

8 What shape is an image dissector?

The silent film era [1] [2]

Before the late 1920s, films did not have sound. Instead written captions were projected showing what the characters were saying. Live music often accompanied silent films. One of the most famous actors of the silent film era was Charlie Chaplin.

Charlie Chaplin

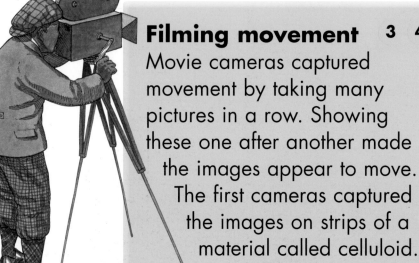

Filming movement [3] [4]

Movie cameras captured movement by taking many pictures in a row. Showing these one after another made the images appear to move. The first cameras captured the images on strips of a material called celluloid.

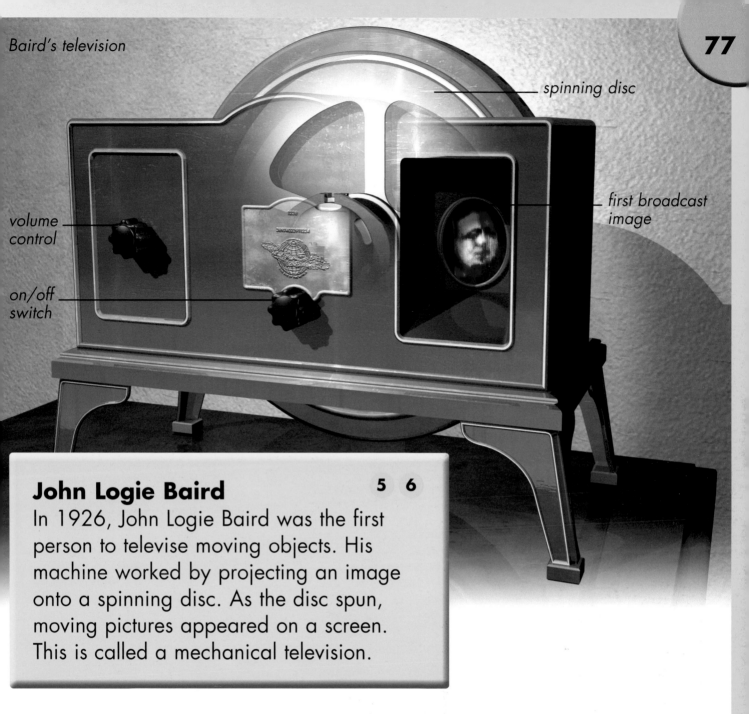

Baird's television

spinning disc

first broadcast image

volume control

on/off switch

John Logie Baird **5 6**

In 1926, John Logie Baird was the first person to televise moving objects. His machine worked by projecting an image onto a spinning disc. As the disc spun, moving pictures appeared on a screen. This is called a mechanical television.

Philo Farnsworth **7 8**

In 1927, the inventor Philo Farnsworth demonstrated his electronic television. Rather than using moving parts, it had a tube-shaped piece of equipment called an image dissector that projected the image onto a screen.

World War I

World War I lasted from 1914 to 1918. At first it was fought by European countries, but by its end, all the world powers had taken part.

1 The French army built trenches. True or false?

2 What was the space between the sides called?

3 What were horse-mounted soldiers called?

4 What were horses also used for?

5 What was the first working tank?

6 At what battle were tanks first used?

7 Where did France build forts?

8 Re-arrange MATOODNUU to spell the name of a French fort.

Trench warfare   1 2

Much of the fighting in Western Europe took place in trenches. After Germany failed to destroy the French army, both sides began to dig trenches, which were defended by troops with machine guns. The space between two opposing sides was called 'no man's land'.

French soldiers defend a trench

French FT-17 tank

machine gun

Horses at war   3 4

Even though engine-powered
vehicles had been invented,
horses were still important.
At the start of the war,
horse-mounted soldiers,
called cavalry, were used.
Large numbers of
horses were also
used to pull
artillery and
ambulances to
the front line.

horse-drawn ambulance

artillery

'Little Willie' tank

Tanks   5 6

The British developed the first
tanks. The earliest working
design was called 'Little
Willie'. Tanks were first used
in combat at the Battle of the
Somme in 1916.

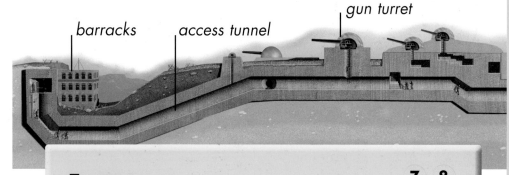

barracks   *access tunnel*   *gun turret*

Forts   7 8

France built forts along its border with
Germany. One of the strongest was Fort
Douaumont at Verdun. However, it was
captured by the Germans in early 1916.

World War II

World War II was the most devastating conflict of all time. In the six years of fighting, from 1939 to 1945, over 50 million people died.

1 In what year did Adolf Hitler's Nazi Party win power?

2 Who invaded Poland in 1939?

3 What does *blitzkrieg* mean in English?

4 What led German *blitzkrieg* attacks?

5 German fighter pilots flew the Messerschmitt Bf 109. True or false?

6 Re-arrange TIEIRPFS for the name of a British fighter plane.

7 Where is Pearl Harbor?

8 What was the V-1?

Adolf Hitler
1 2

In 1933 the Nazi Party won power in Germany and Adolf Hitler became leader. He began to expand Germany's army and take territory from other countries. When it invaded Poland in 1939, Britain and France declared war on Germany.

Blitzkrieg
3 4

The Germans used a style of fighting called *blitzkrieg*, or 'lightning war'. This was a sudden attack, led by tanks. France and the Netherlands were both defeated this way in 1940.

Tiger tank

Battle of Britain **5 6**

In 1940 Germany planned to invade Britain, but to do this they needed to win control of the air. During four months of aerial fighting, British fighter pilots in Spitfires and Hurricanes fought and defeated German Messerschmitt Bf 109s. As a result, Hitler had to give up his plan to invade Britain.

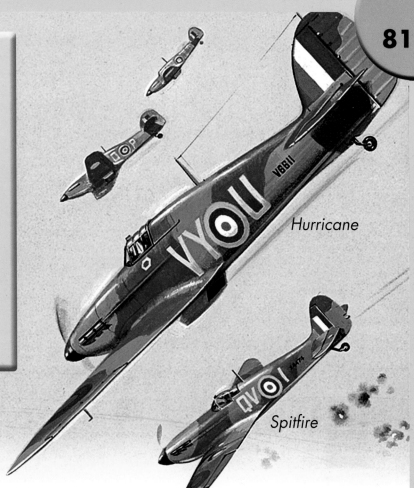

Hurricane

Messerschmitt Bf 109

Spitfire

Japanese attack the US fleet at Pearl Harbor

Pearl Harbor **7**

Japan wanted to destroy the USA's large navy. On 7 December 1941, Japan launched a surprise attack on the US base at Pearl Harbor in Hawaii. The attack caused the USA to declare war on Japan.

Missiles **8**

German scientists developed technology to launch and aim explosive missiles at enemy targets from long distances. The first one to be used in World War II was the V-1 flying bomb in 1944, followed by the V-2 rocket later that year.

V-2 rocket

Europe

After World War II, much of Europe lay in ruins. Initially the West and East were divided. Slowly, countries began to recover. Many joined together to form the European Union.

1 Who built the Berlin Wall?

2 When was the Berlin Wall destroyed?

3 What does the Channel Tunnel connect Britain to?

4 When did the Channel Tunnel open?

5 How many nations are in the EU?

6 Where do EU politicians meet?

7 Unjumble ROEU to spell a currency.

8 In 2002, nine countries started using the euro. True or false?

The Berlin Wall 1 2

The Berlin Wall symbolized the political divide in Europe. Most of Eastern Europe, including East Germany, was controlled by the Soviet Union. In 1961 East Germany started to build a wall in Berlin to stop people leaving for the West. When the Soviet Union collapsed in 1989, the people of Berlin destroyed the Wall.

Channel Tunnel 3 4

To create the tunnel linking Britain to mainland Europe, huge drills called 'tunnel boring machines' were used. It opened in 1994, and is the longest undersea tunnel in the world.

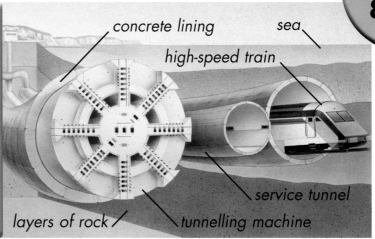

concrete lining   sea

high-speed train

service tunnel

layers of rock   tunnelling machine

European Union 5 6

The 27 nations of the European Union (EU) make up a large political organization. Politicians from the EU countries meet for discussions at the Louise Weiss building in Strasbourg, France.

one euro coin   euro notes

One currency 7 8

On 1 January 2002 a new currency, called the 'euro', was introduced. Initially 12 European Union countries used it, rather than using their own kind of money. Today, 17 countries in the EU use the euro.

Energy sources

Energy sources are divided into nonrenewables and renewables. Nonrenewables will eventually run out, while renewable sources will not.

1 Where is oil and natural gas found?

2 Can oil be found beneath the sea?

3 Coal is a rock. True or false?

4 Where is coal burnt?

5 Unjumble ECUALRN to spell a type of power.

6 What is the most common renewable energy source?

7 What is a group of wind turbines called?

8 Where are wind turbines often placed?

Oil and natural gas   1 2

Underneath the earth there are limited supplies of oil and natural gas. These are collected by drilling. Sometimes the oil and natural gas is beneath the sea. To reach it, platforms are built in the sea. This is called 'offshore drilling'.

Coal 3 4

A common nonrenewable energy source is a type of rock called coal. Coal is dug from the earth and burnt in power stations.

coal

Nuclear 5

Nuclear power is nonrenewable. It works by splitting a metal called uranium. This produces large amounts of heat energy, which causes water to boil, creating steam. This turns a turbine and generates power.

Water 6

When water is used to create power it is called hydroelectricity. Dams are built across rivers to force water to turn a turbine. Water is the most common renewable energy source.

offshore wind farm

generator

gears

blade

Wind 7 8

An important renewable energy source is the wind. It turns large blades, which move a turbine. This generates electricity. Groups of wind turbines are called a wind farm. These are often placed offshore, where the wind is faster.

Protecting the Earth

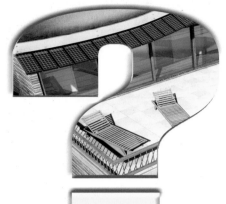

In the last 50 years, there has been growing concern that the Earth needs to be protected from the harmful effects of pollution caused by humans.

1 Is coal a polluting fuel?

2 What heats the Earth?

3 The greenhouse effect means the Earth is cooling. True or false?

4 Do electric cars increase pollution?

5 What type of energy is solar power?

6 What is an eco house?

7 Unjumble SRAGS to spell an eco roofing material.

8 What does recycling mean?

Global warming   1
Many scientists believe that the Earth's temperature has been getting warmer. This process is called 'global warming'. Humans have contributed to this effect by cutting down forests and burning polluting fuels such as coal and oil.

Greenhouse effect   2 3
The Sun's rays heat our planet. Substances in the Earth's atmosphere trap this energy. This is called the 'greenhouse effect'. Pollution in the air means more of this heat is trapped, warming the Earth.

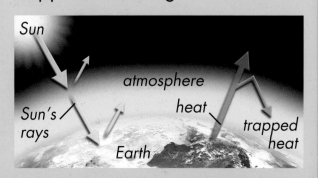

Sun

Sun's rays

atmosphere

heat

trapped heat

Earth

Electric cars   4   5

Most cars run on polluting, non-renewable fuels. However, car-makers have built vehicles that run on electric batteries, which reduce pollution. Cars can also run on renewable energy sources, such as the Sun's rays (solar power).

electric car

wind turbine

solar panel

Eco houses   6   7

Homes that cause very little damage to the planet are called eco houses. They often use solar panels and wind turbines to generate clean, renewable energy. The roof can be covered with grass to keep heat inside the house. Heat can also be taken from the ground.

grass roof

recycling bin

ground source heating pipe

Recycling   8

Recycling means turning the things that we throw away into new materials. Paper, metal and glass can all be recycled.

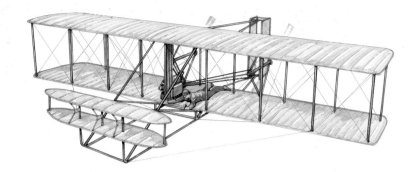

THE MODERN WORLD
History makers

1. World War I started when the heir to the Austrian throne, Franz Ferdinand, was killed in Sarajevo.

2. During World War I around 10 million people died and 21 million were wounded.

3. The first full-length film to contain talking was *The Jazz Singer*, in 1927.

4. Winston Churchill became the British Prime Minister in 1940. He led Britain to victory in World War II.

5. World War II ended in August 1945 when two atomic bombs were dropped on Japan.

6. The first time electricity was generated by a nuclear reactor was in 1951.

7. In 1991 the Soviet Union collapsed. It broke up into separate countries, such as Russia and Belarus.

8. The Channel Tunnel is 50.5km long. The undersea section stretches for 37.9km.

9. The most profitable film of the 20th century was *Titanic*, making more than £1.1 billion.

10. The world's biggest offshore wind farm has 100 turbines. It opened in Britain in 2010.

ANSWERS

Did you get it right? Now it is time to check your answers and see how well you have done! Good luck...

Prehistory

First humans

1 Where did *Homo sapiens* first live?

Answer: Africa

2 When did *Homo sapiens* first leave Africa?

Answer: About 50,000 years ago

3 Where did *Homo sapiens* go next?

Answer: Oceania and southeast Asia

4 What animal group does EARMPTIS spell?

Answer: PRIMATES

5 What is *Homo sapiens'* closest living relation?

Answer: The chimpanzee

6 What was the first type of human called?

Answer: Homo habilis

7 Was fruit eaten by early humans?

Answer: Yes

8 *Homo habilis* ate meat. True or false?

Answer: True

Early tools

1 When did humans first begin making tools?

Answer: Over two million years ago

2 Who made the first tools?

Answer: Homo habilis

3 What were the first tools used for?

Answer: To chop meat and dig up roots

4 Re-arrange NAHD XEA to spell a hunting tool.

Answer: HAND AXE

5 What did *Homo erectus* use to shape stone tools?

Answer: Wood or bone

6 When did the Neanderthals emerge?

Answer: Around 100,000 years ago

7 What was a borer used for?

Answer: To make holes in animal skins

8 Tools were not used to make fire. True or false?

Answer: False, tools were used to make fire

 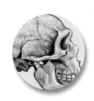

At home

1 What shape were shelters?

Answer: Circular

2 What animal's bones held up the shelters?

Answer: The woolly mammoth's

3 What material covered the shelters?

Answer: Animal skins

4 Where was meat cooked?

Answer: On a spit

5 How did people grind seeds?

Answer: With a heavy stone

6 Where was the first baking done?

Answer: On hot stones or in the ashes of a fire

7 Humans painted wild animals on cave walls. True or false?

Answer: True

8 Re-arrange RCHOE to spell a coloured clay.

Answer: OCHRE

Hunting

1 A spear is sharp. True or false?

Answer: True

2 Did people hunt large animals alone?

Answer: No, they worked together

3 The mammoth is the size of what modern animal?

Answer: The elephant

4 What parts of the woolly mammoth did people use?

Answer: Meat, skins and tusks

5 Fish hooks are made of what?

Answer: Bone, stone or wood

6 Unjumble RHOAPNO to spell a tool.

Answer: HARPOON

7 When was the bow and arrow first used?

Answer: About 18,000 years ago

8 What did it allow people to do?

Answer: Hunt from a distance

Farming

1 When did farming first begin?

Answer: Around 10,000 years ago

2 Where is Mesopotamia?

Answer: In the Middle East

3 Which rivers fed the farms of Mesopotamia?

Answer: The Tigris and Euphrates

4 What type of plants are cereals?

Answer: Grasses

5 Re-arrange ZEIAM to spell a type of cereal.

Answer: MAIZE

6 Houses in Skara Brae are made of what material?

Answer: Stone

7 Where is Skara Brae?

Answer: In the Orkney Islands

8 People kept sheep on Skara Brae. True or false?

Answer: True

Metal work

1 Re-arrange ZEBNRO to spell a metal.

Answer: BRONZE

2 Where did the Bronze Age begin?

Answer: In Europe and Asia

3 Bronze is made of which two metals?

Answer: Copper and tin

4 Why was bronze used to make weapons?

Answer: It keeps a sharp edge

5 Bronze was not used to make bracelets. True or false?

Answer: False, bronze was made into jewellery, such as bracelets

6 Why did people use iron instead of bronze?

Answer: It was easier to mine

7 Why is iron useful?

Answer: It is strong and easy to sharpen

8 Name a weapon made of iron.

Answer: A sword

Ancient worlds

The Sumerians

1 Which two rivers run through the fertile crescent?

Answer: The Tigris and Euphrates

2 Sumer lies in what modern country?

Answer: Iraq

3 Ur was a large city. True or false?

Answer: True

4 What was at the centre of Ur?

Answer: The Great Ziggurat

5 What did the Sumerians write with?

Answer: A stylus

6 What writing system did the Sumerians use?

Answer: Cuneiform script

7 Unjumble HWELE to spell a Sumerian invention.

Answer: WHEEL

8 What did the Sumerians first use the wheel for?

Answer: To shape pottery

Pharaohs

1 Who was in charge of the army and government?

Answer: The pharaoh

2 The pharaohs were believed to be gods. True or false?

Answer: True

3 Who uses a crook?

Answer: A shepherd

4 What is used to harvest grain?

Answer: A flail

5 What is the name of the falcon god?

Answer: Horus

6 How were the bodies preserved?

Answer: They were mummified

7 What was removed from the pharaoh's body after he died?

Answer: The stomach, liver, lungs and intestines

8 Re-arrange HPSSUAAGOCR to spell a stone container.

Answer: SARCOPHAGUS

Pyramid building

1 How many pyramids are there at Giza?

Answer: Three

2 The Great Pyramid took 200 years to build. True or false?

Answer: False, it took 20 years to build

3 How many stone blocks are in the Great Pyramid?

Answer: Over two million

4 How many craftsmen shaped the stone blocks?

Answer: Around 4,000

5 What tools did the craftsmen use?

Answer: Pickaxes, hammers and chisels

6 How were the blocks moved?

Answer: On a sledge

7 How many workers built a pyramid?

Answer: Around 6,700

8 Unjumble SANOCTEP to spell a pyramid-shaped stone.

Answer: CAPSTONE

Olympic Games

1 When did the Olympic Games probably begin?

Answer: 776 BCE

2 How often were the Olympic Games?

Answer: Every four years

3 Who was Zeus?

Answer: The king of the Greek gods

4 Olympia is in northeast Greece. True or false?

Answer: False, it is in the southwest

5 What was the statue of Zeus at Olympia made of?

Answer: Mostly ivory and gold

6 What was the first event at the Olympic Games?

Answer: Sprinting

7 Unjumble CSIDSU to spell an event.

Answer: DISCUS

8 What was the woman-only event held at Olympia called?

Answer: The Heraean Games

The Romans

1 What did most Romans wear every day?

Answer: A plain tunic

2 What is a toga?

Answer: A cloth wrapped around the body

3 What did Roman soldiers wear?

Answer: Metal armour and helmets

4 Wealthy Romans bought slaves. True or false?

Answer: True

5 What was the centre of a town called?

Answer: The forum

6 Where did most Romans live?

Answer: In apartment blocks

7 Did wealthy Romans eat lying down at feasts?

Answer: Yes, they lay on couches

8 Unjumble RMODOSEU to spell a favourite Roman food.

Answer: DORMOUSE

The ancient Chinese

1 Why was the Great Wall built?

Answer: To defend China from attack

2 When did building start on the Wall?

Answer: In the 5th century BCE

3 What was the Great Wall's total length?

Answer: About 8,850km

4 Re-arrange PERPA to spell a chinese invention.

Answer: PAPER

5 How was the wheelbarrow used?

Answer: To carry heavy weights

6 Terracotta is a type of clay. True or false?

Answer: True

7 What did most ancient Chinese peasants work as?

Answer: Farmers

8 Where did peasants sell their produce?

Answer: At town markets

The Mayans

1 Mayan pyramids have steps.
True or false?

Answer: True

2 What was at the top of many
Mayan pyramids?

Answer: A temple or an observatory

3 What colour was Chichén Itzá?

Answer: Red

4 What was the ball game called?

Answer: Pok-a-tok

5 How many teams played in the
Mayan ball game?

Answer: Two teams

6 Unjumble UBRBRE to spell
a material.

Answer: RUBBER

7 Who was the most important
Mayan god?

Answer: Itzamna

8 Did the Mayans make
human sacrifices?

Answer: Yes, sometimes

The Celts

1 What were Celtic houses called?

Answer: Roundhouses

2 What shape were the roofs?

Answer: Cone shaped

3 Where in the house was the fire?

Answer: In the middle

4 Where did the Celts place their forts?

Answer: On hills

5 Re-arrange CDSTIHE to spell
something the Celts built for
protection.

Answer: DITCHES

6 The Celts had many gods.
True or false?

Answer: True

7 What were the Celts' main
weapons?

Answer: The sword and shield

8 What colour did warriors in Britain
paint themselves?

Answer: Blue

The Middle Ages

The Vikings

1 Viking warriors used war axes. True or false?

Answer: True

2 What did rich Vikings wear in battle?

Answer: Helmets and chainmail

3 What is chainmail?

Answer: A type of armour made of small, linked metal rings

4 Where did they set up trade routes?

Answer: All over Europe

5 Re-arrange OYEHN to spell an item Vikings traded.

Answer: HONEY

6 What were Viking boats called?

Answer: Longships

7 Which two large islands did the Vikings discover?

Answer: Iceland and Greenland

8 What did the Vikings call North America?

Answer: Vinland

The Normans

1 When was the Battle of Hastings?

Answer: 14 October 1066

2 The English fought on horses. True or false?

Answer: False, they fought on foot

3 What was the name of the English king killed at Hastings?

Answer: Harold

4 What is the Bayeux Tapestry made of?

Answer: Cloth

5 How long is the Bayeux Tapestry?

Answer: Nearly 70 metres

6 What type of castle did the Normans build in England?

Answer: Motte-and-bailey

7 What was the tower on top of the motte called?

Answer: The keep

8 Re-arrange LBIEYA to spell the fenced area of a castle.

Answer: BAILEY

Castles

1 What was the most common type of castle?

Answer: A keep

2 What made a keep harder to attack?

Answer: Walls built around it

3 Why were towers added to castles?

Answer: For defence

4 What would defenders shoot from high walls?

Answer: Arrows

5 Cold oil was tipped onto attackers. True or false?

Answer: False, the oil was boiling hot

6 Re-arrange RLASO to spell the name of a castle room.

Answer: SOLAR

7 What part of the castle did the lord and lady live in?

Answer: The main tower

8 Who lived at the top of the tower?

Answer: The lady's servants

The Black Death

1 What probably caused the Black Death?

Answer: Bubonic plague

2 Unjumble ELFA to spell an insect.

Answer: FLEA

3 How did humans become infected with the plague?

Answer: From flea bites

4 How did people try to stop it from spreading?

Answer: Quarantine

5 What were the dead buried in?

Answer: In plague pits

6 Where did the Black Death spread quickly?

Answer: In towns

7 Towns had modern toilets. True or false?

Answer: False

8 Where did people throw their waste?

Answer: Onto the street

The Incas

1 What decorated Inca headdresses?

Answer: Feathers

2 Only Inca women wore jewellery. True or false?

Answer: False, Inca men and women wore jewellery

3 What was the sun god called?

Answer: Inti

4 Re-arrange AAMM LAIQUL to spell out the name of the Inca moon goddess.

Answer: MAMA QUILLA

5 What was the ceremonial knife called?

Answer: The tumi

6 What were houses made from?

Answer: Stone

7 What country is Machu Picchu in?

Answer: Peru

8 When was Machu Picchu built?

Answer: In the 15th century

The samurai

1 What was the most important weapon?

Answer: The katana

2 Re-arrange ZSKWAAIIH to spell out the name of a samurai weapon.

Answer: WAKIZASHI

3 The *naginata* is a short, blunt pole. True or false?

Answer: False, it is a long pole topped with a curved blade

4 How were samurai meant to be towards their masters?

Answer: Obedient and loyal

5 What does *Bushido* mean?

Answer: The way of the warrior

6 What did samurai wear to protect themselves in battle?

Answer: Armour

7 What was samurai armour made of?

Answer: Leather and iron

8 What decorated samurai helmets?

Answer: Antlers

Exploration and empire

Explorers

1 Who paid for Columbus's voyage?

Answer: Queen Isabella of Spain

2 On what date did Columbus land in the Bahamas?

Answer: 12 October 1492

3 What does *conquistadors* mean?

Answer: Conquerors

4 Who attacked the Aztec Empire?

Answer: Hernán Cortés

5 Re-arrange ALMGNLEA to spell an explorer's name.

Answer: MAGELLAN

6 Where was Magellan killed?

Answer: The Philippines

7 What was the name of da Gama's ship?

Answer: São Gabriel

8 Da Gama sailed around America. True or false?

Answer: False, he sailed around Africa and landed in India

Pirates

1 What ships did pirates attack?

Answer: Merchant ships

2 What was Edward Teach known as?

Answer: Blackbeard

3 Who got the biggest share of the loot?

Answer: The pirate captain

4 Rich prisoners were held for ransom. True or false?

Answer: True

5 Re-arrange YLJLO OREGR to spell the name of the flag pirate ships flew.

Answer: JOLLY ROGER

6 What was the most famous design of a pirate flag?

Answer: A white skull and cross-bones

7 Which captain buried his treasure?

Answer: William Kidd

8 Where was Kidd's treasure buried?

Answer: Gardiners Island

Slavery

1 Where were most slaves taken from?

Answer: The west coast of Africa

2 What ocean did many slaves cross?

Answer: The Atlantic Ocean

3 Where in Africa did Arab slave traders work?

Answer: East Africa

4 Unjumble LDGO to spell a trade item.

Answer: GOLD

5 Where did the Arab traders sell their slaves?

Answer: In the Middle East and North Africa

6 What was cotton used to make?

Answer: Cloth

7 Abolitionists wanted to end slavery. True or false?

Answer: True

8 What year was slavery ended in the United States?

Answer: 1865

Kings and queens

1 How many wives did Henry VIII have?

Answer: Six

2 Who was Henry VIII's first wife?

Answer: Catherine of Aragon

3 What was Elizabeth I also known as?

Answer: The Virgin Queen

4 What year was the Spanish Armada defeated?

Answer: 1588

5 Re-arrange YAMR UATRST to spell the name of William of Orange's wife.

Answer: MARY STUART

6 When did William arrive in England?

Answer: In 1689

7 What year was the Battle of the Boyne?

Answer: 1690

8 Louis XVI was executed in 1693. True or false?

Answer: False, his execution was in 1793

Age of Revolution

1 There were 14 American colonies. True or false?

Answer: False, there were 13

2 Which empire did the colonies fight?

Answer: The British empire

3 What country did the colonies form?

Answer: The United States of America

4 What year did the French Revolution start?

Answer: 1789

5 Who ruled France after Louis XVI?

Answer: The National Convention

6 Unjumble LUETNOLGII to spell a device.

Answer: GUILLOTINE

7 Who was Simón Bolívar?

Answer: A revolutionary leader in South America

8 By what date had most of South America won independence?

Answer: 1829

The Napoleonic Wars

1 Where was Napoleon born?

Answer: Corsica

2 What year did he become emperor?

Answer: 1804

3 What was Napoleon's most famous victory?

Answer: The Battle of Austerlitz

4 Napoleon invaded Britain. True or false?

Answer: False, he lost to the British navy

5 What country did France invade in 1812?

Answer: Russia

6 In what year did Napoleon fight his last battle?

Answer: 1815

7 Where did this battle take place?

Answer: Waterloo

8 Unjumble APISURS to spell a country at the battle.

Answer: PRUSSIA

Industrial Revolution

1 Who invented the spinning jenny?

Answer: James Hargreaves

2 What did Richard Arkwright invent?

Answer: The spinning frame

3 What was at the centre of towns?

Answer: Factories

4 Where did the workers live?

Answer: In cottages, close to the factory

5 Why were canals built?

Answer: So boats could transport goods

6 Young children often had to work in factories. True or false?

Answer: True

7 Unjumble ESMAT to spell a type of power.

Answer: STEAM

8 When did Robert Stephenson build the *Rocket*?

Answer: 1829

Expanding empires

1 In what century did Europeans rush to control Africa?

Answer: The 19th century

2 Belgium owned land in Africa. True or false?

Answer: True

3 Unjumble CIAVIROT to spell a British queen.

Answer: VICTORIA

4 What was the largest empire?

Answer: The British empire

5 Where was David Livingstone from?

Answer: Scotland

6 In what year did Livingstone see the Victoria Falls?

Answer: 1855

7 In which continent was most of the French empire?

Answer: Africa

8 What was the Foreign Legion?

Answer: A French army unit

The modern world

First flight

1 What was the name of the monk who flew a glider?

Answer: Eilmer of Malmesbury

2 What did da Vinci draw plans of?

Answer: A hang glider and a helicopter

3 Who made the first powered flight?

Answer: The Wright brothers

4 When was the first powered flight made?

Answer: In 1903

5 Unjumble PMNOONLAE to spell an aeroplane.

Answer: MONOPLANE

6 When did Blériot cross the Channel?

Answer: In 1909

7 Who created the first airship?

Answer: Henri Giffard

8 Aeroplanes were used in World War I. True or false?

Answer: True

Submarines

1 How were the first submarines powered?

Answer: By hand

2 Unjumble GMRESARU to spell an early submarine.

Answer: RESURGAM

3 What powers the largest submarines?

Answer: Nuclear power

4 What was the name of the first nuclear submarine?

Answer: USS Nautilus

5 Submersibles are very large. True or false?

Answer: False, they are very small

6 Can submersibles be remote controlled?

Answer: Yes

7 What is a bathyscaphe?

Answer: A deep-diving vessel

8 How deep did the *Trieste* dive?

Answer: More than 10,000 metres

Films and TV

Before the 1920s films had sound. True or false?

Answer: False, they were silent

Unjumble EHCRIAL LNIPCAH to spell an actor's name.

Answer: CHARLIE CHAPLIN

What was used to capture movement?

Answer: A movie camera

What material was used to make films?

Answer: Celluloid

In what year did Baird first televise moving objects?

Answer: 1926

What was projected onto a spinning disc?

Answer: An image

Did Farnsworth's television use moving parts?

Answer: No

What shape is an image dissector?

Answer: Tube shaped

World War I

1 The French army built trenches. True or false?

Answer: True

2 What was the space between the sides called?

Answer: No man's land

3 What were horse-mounted soldiers called?

Answer: Cavalry

4 What were horses also used for?

Answer: Pulling artillery and ambulances to the front line

5 What was the first working tank?

Answer: Little Willie

6 At what battle were tanks first used?

Answer: The Battle of the Somme

7 Where did France build forts?

Answer: Along its border with Germany

8 Re-arrange MATOODNUU to spell the name of a French fort.

Answer: DOUAUMONT

World War II

1 In what year did Adolf Hitler's Nazi Party win power?

Answer: 1933

2 Who invaded Poland in 1939?
Answer: Germany

3 What does *blitzkrieg* mean in English?

Answer: Lightning war

4 What led German *blitzkrieg* attacks?

Answer: Tanks

5 German fighter pilots flew the Messerschmitt Bf 109. True or false?

Answer: True

6 Re-arrange TIEIRPFS for the name of a British fighter plane.

Answer: SPITFIRE

7 Where is Pearl Harbor?

Answer: Hawaii

8 What was the V-1?

Answer: A flying bomb

Europe

1 Who built the Berlin Wall?

Answer: East Germany

2 When was the Berlin Wall destroyed?

Answer: 1989

3 What does the Channel Tunnel connect Britain to?

Answer: Mainland Europe

4 When did the Channel Tunnel open?

Answer: 1994

5 How many nations are in the EU?

Answer: 27

6 Where do EU politicians meet?

Answer: At the Louise Weiss building, Strasbourg

7 Unjumble ROEU to spell a currency.

Answer: EURO

8 In 2002 nine countries started using the euro. True or false?

Answer: False, it was 12

Energy sources

1 Where is oil and natural gas found?

Answer: Underneath the earth

2 Can oil be found beneath the sea?

Answer: Yes

3 Coal is a rock. True or false?

Answer: True

4 Where is coal burnt?

Answer: In power stations

5 Unjumble ECUALRN to spell a type of power.

Answer: NUCLEAR

6 What is the most common renewable energy source.

Answer: Hydroelectricity

7 What is a group of wind turbines called?

Answer: A wind farm

8 Where are wind turbines often placed?

Answer: Offshore

Protecting the Earth

1 Is coal a polluting fuel?

Answer: Yes

2 What heats the Earth?

Answer: The Sun's rays

3 The greenhouse effect means the Earth is cooling. True or false?

Answer: False, the Earth is warming up

4 Do electric cars increase pollution?

Answer: No, they reduce it

5 What type of energy is solar power?

Answer: Renewable

6 What is an eco house?

Answer: A home that causes little damage to the planet

7 Unjumble SRAGS to spell an eco roofing material.

Answer: GRASS

8 What does recycling mean?

Answer: Turning what we throw away into new materials

Words to know

Alliance An agreement between countries to help each other. They are often used when countries decide to fight together against a shared enemy.

Americas A large land mass that is made up of North and South America.

Atmosphere A layer of different gases that surrounds a planet.

Australopithecus An ape-like animal that first lived in Africa around four million years ago. Many scientists believe humans evolved from this creature.

BCE It stands for 'Before the Common Era' or 'Before the Christian Era', and counts down towards the year that Jesus was born (1 CE).

Bronze Age A period of human civilization when people widely used the metal bronze for tools and weapons. It started around 5,000 years ago, after the Stone Age.

Catholic Church The largest, and oldest, Christian church. Its leader is called the Pope.

CE It stands for 'Common Era' or 'Christian Era', and counts up from the year that Jesus was born to the present day.

Colony An area of land under the control of another state.

Compass A tool used to find out geographic direction. The magnetized needle always points north.

Continent One of the main large areas of land on Earth: Africa, Antarctica, Asia, Australia, Europe, North America and South America.

Criminals People who have broken the law.

Diesel A type of fuel that is made from petroleum. It is used to power engines.

Domesticate When humans tame or control an animal or plant.

Electricity The charge of small particles called electrons and protons, which is used to power machines and other devices.

Emperor A powerful male ruler who controls an area of land called an empire.

Evolve Where a species develops new or different features. Evolution takes thousands of years.

Fertile Land that is very good for growing crops.

Fort A military building or structure that is used to defend an area.

Homo erectus The scientific name of a human ancestor that first lived around 1.8 million years ago and was the first to walk upright on two legs.

Homo habilis The scientific name of a human ancestor that lived around two million years ago and was one of the first species to make simple tools out of stone.

Homo sapiens The scientific name for humans. *Homo sapiens* first evolved in Africa around 200,000 years ago.

Independent A person, group, territory or organization that is not controlled by anyone else.

Iron Age A period of human civilization when people first widely used iron for making tools and weapons. It started around 4,000 years ago, after the Bronze Age.

Merchant ship A type of ship that is used to carry items for buying and selling.

Mesopotamia An area of land centred on the Tigris and Euphrates rivers, located mostly in modern-day Iraq.

Middle East A region that covers western Asia and parts of North Africa. It is also known as the Near East.

Missile An object that is thrown or launched as a weapon.

Nazi Party The name of the political party that ruled Germany from 1933 to 1945. Led by Adolf Hitler, the Nazi Party believed that the white race was superior to other racial groups.

Neanderthal An extinct human-like creature that lived between 200,000 and 30,000 years ago. They could walk upright, make tools, hunt and control fire.

Nuclear The energy produced by the splitting of a tiny particle called an atom. It can be used for generating power or as a weapon.

Observatory A building or structure that is used to examine the sky or the stars, usually with very large and powerful telescopes.

Plague A disease that spreads quickly and usually causes death to humans.

Pollution When people release harmful items into the environment.

Settlement A place where people live together. They can be as large as a city or as small as a group of homes.

Shrine A place where a god, saint, or person is worshipped or remembered.

Slave A person who is owned by another person and has to work for them.

Soviet Union A large state made up of several different countries, including Russia. The Soviet Union began in 1922 and ended in 1991.

Steam The gas produced when water is boiled. It is used as a source of power.

Stone Age A period of human civilization that started around three million years ago when people widely used stone for making tools and weapons.

Survey The careful study of an area or subject.

Tank A heavy armoured vehicle that moves on tracks, armed with a cannon.

Temple A building where people pray and carry out religious ceremonies.

Territory An area of land or part of a larger country.

Tool An object that is used to complete a job or task.

Traders People who buy, sell or swap different things. They often travel long distances to trade with other people.

Tribe A group of people or families that join together, in small or large numbers.

Turbine An engine that works by capturing the power of moving steam, wind or water. This makes the turbine spin and that motion is used to generate energy.

Vessel A craft, such as a boat, built to travel on water.

Index

Acknowledgements

The Publisher would like to thank the following for permission to reproduce their material.
Every care has been taken to trace copyright holders. However, if there have been
unintentional omissions or failure to trace copyright holders, we apologize and
will, if informed, endeavour to make corrections in any future edition.

Top = t; Bottom = b; Centre = c; Left = l; Right = r

Page: 15 Alamy/Hitendra Sinkar; 17 Corbis/Adam Woofitt; 26 Shutterstock/Dan Breckwoldt;
29 Shutterstock/Sadequl Hussain; 35 Shutterstock/Kamira; 43 Getty/Bridgeman Art Library;
49 Shutterstock/Amy Nichole Harris; 59 Shutterstock/Brzostowa; 74 Corbis/Hulton Deutsch;
75 Corbis/Jeff Rotman; 77 Corbis/Bettmann; 83c Shutterstock/AND Inc.;
83bl Shutterstock/Matt Trommer; 83br Shutterstock/Christina Solodukhina;
85cl Shutterstock/Kletr; 85cr Shutterstock/Alex Uralsky; 87 Corbis/Car Culture